Viva Oaxaca

An Insider's Guide to Oaxaca's Charms

CONTENTS

Introduction	3
Best times to come	5
Semana Santa	5
Guelegüetza	6
Day of the Dead	7
The Christmas season	9
What to see and do in Oaxaca	12
Out and about	17
Monte Albán	17
The route to Mitla	18
Teotitlán del Valle	19
South to Ocotlán	21
Southwest to Zaachila	24
Northwest of Oaxaca	26
Where to stay	26
Where to eat	32
Fine dining	33
Comida tipica—Oaxacan food	39
Comida corrida—fixed price meals	41
Non-Oaxacan cuisine	43
Outside of Oaxaca	45
Coffee, chocolate and pastries	50
Street food	53
Map of Oaxaca (west/east of *zócalo*)	47-48
Entertainment	55
Shopping	57
Getting to Oaxaca	64
Getting around	66
Classes—Spanish, cooking, dance, exercise	69
Eco-tourism	74
Mezcall!	75
What you'll need in Oaxaca	78
Health and medical matters	78
The dozen best things to do in Oaxaca	83
Facts, figures and handy things to know	84
Market days	91
Disappointments	91
A note about giving	92
Index	96

Introduction

Viva Oaxaca is the book we wish had existed before we first came to Oaxaca. After our many extended stays here, we've included nearly everything useful we've learned about the city and its surroundings. It's our hope that *Viva Oaxaca* will help you make the most of your time in this remarkable place.

Oaxaca is a kaleidoscope. It's colorful, bustling, vibrating with life from early morning until late at night. It can also be reserved, formal, and mysterious — hiding some of its most intriguing features behind its high stone walls, weathered doors, and the gracious manners of its citizens.

With a little Spanish, you might be on first-name terms with a friendly Oaxacan in a few minutes. You'll soon be responding to the courtly farewell, *"¡Que le vaya bien!"*—may it go well with you—with an equally polite *"¡Igualmente!"*—the same to you.

Yet you could also live here for years and never quite reach the heart of the place. You can get a taste of Oaxaca in a day, see most of its major attractions in a week or two, and yet, like us, return year after year and still be intrigued and surprised. And of course, Oaxaca is a living city that continues to grow and change.

Santo Domingo church   photo by Elissa Rubinstein

Many people come to Oaxaca to escape a cold northern winter. Oaxaca's climate from October through February is ideal -- seldom too hot or too cold, and drenched in sunshine. It gets quite hot later in the spring, but in summer and fall, afternoon rain showers refresh and cool the region.

We quickly learned not to expect resort-style perfection here. Only if you stay behind the walls of one of the de luxe hotels, such as the **Camino Real** or **Casa Oaxaca**, will your world be calm and orderly. The minute you venture out, you'll be in the midst of life as it's really lived here--bustling, colorful and noisy. Oaxaca is a city with a great deal to offer, and it's not here just for tourists. It's a bustling, vibrant, growing and constantly changing Mexican city.

Oaxaca is full of contrasts. Many of its grand colonial buildings have been beautifully restored, but others are crumbling or splattered with graffiti. It's a joy to stroll the **Alcalá** (also known as the *Andador Turistico*), the ***zócalo***, and other pedestrian zones, but a few steps away you'll be jostling through crowds of *Oaxaqueños*, dodging speeding buses, and navigating the city's poorly maintained, often treacherous sidewalks.

Like its seven famous *mole* (pronounced MOH lay) sauces, Oaxaca is a rich mix of contrasting ingredients. The steps of the awe-inspiring **Santo Domingo Church,** the heart of Oaxaca's **UNESCO World Heritage Site**, are also a favorite spot for teenagers to hang out and young lovers to make out. The ***zócalo***, the great laurel-shaded square at the center of the city, isn't just a spot for a snack or a cup of coffee, Oaxaca's cinnamon-laced hot chocolate, or ***mezcal***; it's also a non-stop crafts market, a concert hall, and a stage for strolling minstrels, raucous street theater, and frequent political protests.

You'll soon realize that in Oaxaca it's normal for everything to be jumbled together into a vivid, noisy pastiche. A few years ago, we were enjoying a free Sunday concert by the **State Band of Oaxaca.** Just as the band reached the climax of the 1812 Overture, complete with clanging bells from atop the nearby **Cathedral,** a *calenda* (procession) from a local church marched by, going *mano-a-mano* against the band with their own tubas, trumpets and drums. Nobody was bothered, and the band didn't miss a beat; it was just another rich taste of *la vida Oaxaqueña*.

Best times to come: a calendar of events and attractions

The celebration that draws thousands of visitors to Oaxaca every spring is **Semana Santa**, the holy week before Easter Sunday.

The entire 40 days of Lent are packed with religious pageantry in Oaxaca and surrounding towns. The most striking single event is the eerie **Procession of Silence** in Oaxaca on Good Friday, when purple- and white-hooded penitents file through the streets in somber ranks. Also on Good Friday, a passion play takes place in the pueblo of Zaachila. Later that evening, back in Oaxaca, the Virgin is carried in solemn procession around Soledad Basílica.

The Processsion of Silence- Photo by Kim Elinski

Oaxaca's unique cultural mix is on display in the magnificent **Danza de la Pluma**, Dance of the Feathers, held at **Carmen Alto Church** on Easter Sunday. The colorfully costumed dancers re-enact the Spanish Conquest of Mexico in the early 1500s and the conversion of Mexico's indigenous population to Catholicism.

The Easter season in Oaxaca also includes the lovely **Samaritana**, on the fourth Friday of Lent, when locals graciously offer delicious drinks to passers-by. The best places to see this are at the Cathedral, the major churches, the Panuelito, and in the nearby neighborhoods of Xochimilco and Jalatlaco (*Viva Oaxaca's* cover captures the spirit of *La Samaritana*.)

On Thursday of the week before Easter, throngs of devoted locals make a pilgrimage to all seven churches of the city. During the morning of Good Friday, many communities, including nearby Xochimilco and the Ex-Marquesado, plus Teotitlán del Valle and Tlacochahuaya, celebrate *El Encuentro*--the last meeting between Jesus and his mother--with poignant processions.

The *Guelaguetza*, Oaxaca's huge folkloric dance festival, spans eight days starting on the Monday after July 16. Indigenous groups from the State of Oaxaca's seven regions flood the city to present their traditional music and dances in intricate, colorful costumes. It's a week packed with festivity and celebration, not even counting the *mezcal* festival that adds to the revelry.

The main shows take place on two successive Mondays at the **Guelaguetza Auditorium on Fortín hill** overlooking the city, which may sport a modernistic fabric roof by 2012. Tickets are sold at the Museum of Oaxacan Painters at Independencia 607, and at the Teatro Macedonio Alcalá at Independencia 900, but we suggest purchasing them well in advance from the state tourist office (about $40 U.S. each). Email infooax@yahoo.com.mx for information. Tickets are also available through Ticketmaster, www.ticketmaster.com.mx, or by calling +52 555 325 9000.

During the last week of July and the first week of August, Oaxaca hosts two weeks of **classical music**. Musicians from all over the world give master classes, direct student concerts and give concerts on their own. Details at www.oaxacacalendar.com/.

Early morning at Oaxaca's Soledad Basílica

October is a great time to visit Oaxaca. In the middle of the month, Oaxaca hosts its **Festival de Otoño** honoring the late conductor Eduardo Mata. Several musical or dance events take place every day for five days, many of them for free. We've attended some world-class concerts during this festival.

At the end of October, visitors flood Oaxaca for **El Día de los Muertos**, the **Day of the Dead**. Imaginative skeletons, exquisite sand paintings, flowers, candles, special foods, and lovingly constructed altars appear everywhere as locals prepare to commune with loved ones who have died. The smell of *cempazuchitl* (marigolds) fills the air, and their distinctive colors adorn altars and gravesites. Reflecting a uniquely Mexican view of life and death, it's a joyful rather than a somber time.

The old and new cemeteries of the nearby city of Xoxocotlán are extremely evocative, and heavily visited by tourists. Other events, including *comparsas*—processions with fantastically costumed figures—take place in town and in nearby Etla.

The most important, and touching, period starts in the late afternoon of October 31. That's when *angelitos*—the spirits of dead children—revisit their families. From then through the afternoon of November 2, families gather in cemeteries, decorate the graves of relatives, and bring food, drink and beloved objects to share as they commune with their *fieles difuntos*—the faithful dead.

Visitors can experience this beautiful tradition, whose roots lie deep in the pre-Hispanic past,

He loved to read—Day of the Dead figure

at cemeteries in the nearby towns of **Xoxocotlán, Santa María Atzompa, Zaachila, San Antonio Etla, San Felipe del Agua**, and, in northern Oaxaca state, **Tuxtepec.** In the city of Oaxaca, the **San Miguel Cemetery (or *Panteón General*)** has a much lower-key observance.

So many people visit Xoxocotlán on the Day of the Dead that it's taken on a bit of a carnival aspect. We suggest going to the cemetery of Santa Maria Atzompa instead. It's much less crowded than Xoxocotlán, and the vistas of candlelit graves with city lights in the background are enchanting,

This is a good time to use the services of local guides. They will know where and when events are taking place, and get you there. Oaxaca's hotels will be full, so book your lodging well in advance.

Music lovers are drawn to to Oaxaca's **International Organ and Early Music Festival**, which can take place in the spring or fall.

The state of Oaxaca is home to 24 organs built before 1776, eight of which have been lovingly restored. The annual festival draws world-class musicians who give master classes, lectures, and concerts on these beautiful instruments. Detailed information at: http://iohio.org.mx/en/index.htm.

Oaxaca has now hosted its first ever **International Independent Film and Video Festival**, thanks toChr its creator, Ramiz Azar and his talented wife, Diana.

Dancing figure at Casa de Las artesanías

The first festival—a smash hit--took place in mid- November, 2010. Ramiz tells us that the 2011 edition will be even bigger and better.

The **Christmas season** is our favorite time to be in Oaxaca. The weather is beautiful; cool at night, but warm and sunny almost every day. Churches sponsor lovely candlelit processions led by children dressed as Mary and Joseph, accompanied by musicians, fireworks, and huge, fanciful paper-maché figures called *gigantes* (giants) or *mojigangas,* each animated by a person hidden inside.

The **Virgen de la Soledad**, Oaxaca's patron, is fêted up to and including December 18. Avenida Independencia, the street leading to **Soledad Basílica**, is packed with stands selling food and crafts. On the night of the 17th, Soledad's revered statue of the Virgin is paraded around the churchyard on a flower-draped pallet, preceded by bejeweled, 18-foot-tall banners. Not to be missed!

Oaxaca's pre-Christmas festivities also include the famous **Noche de Rábanos,** the **Night of the Radishes.** On December 23, the zócalo is filled with displays of intricate and imaginative creations —churches, processions, village festivals, farmers, sorcerers, musicians, nativity scenes, you name it — fashioned entirely of carved giant radishes, corn husks, or dried straw flowers.

We've tried to convince skeptical friends how striking and enchanting these creations are. Come and see for yourself.

Nativity scene from the Night of the Radishes

Warning: Get there well before the official opening or plan to stand in line for hours. Serious photographers or viewers should arrive before 11 am, when you can get close to these evanescent works of art as they're being assembled. By 2 pm, you'll be moved farther away, but you can still get good shots with a telephoto lens. By 7 pm every table in every café at the zócalo is taken, and even walking through the zócalo becomes difficult (later in the evening it's impossible!). If you really want to be able to see the displays, get to the zócalo before 3 pm. **Rábanos** is one of Oaxaca's not-to-be-missed celebrations.

On the nights leading up to Christmas, and culminating on **Noche Buena** (Christmas Eve), churches and other groups sponsor posadas. Throngs of the faithful (often joined by foreign visitors) go from door to door carrying candles, singing traditional songs, and asking for *posada* (shelter), only to be ritually turned away time and again until they are finally taken in. Colorful, often beautiful, floats converge at the *zócalo* starting at around 8:30 pm.

Angelitos--little angels--grace a float on Christmas Eve

Oaxaca's Christmas festivities actually continue through the 2nd of February. *Los Reyes Magos* (the Three Wise Men) deliver presents not on Christmas Eve but on Janurary 6. On that day, Oaxacans consume special ring-shaped breads (*roscas*) that hide tiny dolls symbolizing the Baby Jesus. If you find a doll in your piece, you get to provide *tamales* and *atole* to everyone present on Candlemas, the final evening of the holidays, on February 2.

In an attempt to encourage tourism to Oaxaca, the authorities have created a new tradition, the **Noche de Luces,** Night of Lights. Once a month, on the Saturday evening that falls on or before the 15th, the center of town vibrates with music, dance and other presentations in a number of venues, mostly for free. In addition, many businesses stay open late and offer bargains.

For an excellent listing of current events, upcoming events, and museums and galleries in and around Oaxaca, check out Margie Barclay's up-to-the-minute **calendar:** http://oaxacacalendar.com/.

What to see and do in Oaxaca

Oaxaca has more than twenty churches and ex-convents, most of which are of architectural, artistic, and photographic interest. The star, however, is the 16th-Century **Santo Domingo de Guzmán**, on the pedestrianized Alcalá. The Renaissance façade of the church is striking, changing its mood hour by hour with the shifting light. The inside, described as "exuberant baroque," is overwhelming, with acres of gold leaf and religious iconography. Don't miss the exquisite gilded chapel to the right of the main entrance, or the remarkable family tree of the church's namesake saint on the ceiling just above the entrance. We recommend a guided tour to help you truly appreciate this UNESCO World Heritage site.

The beautifully restored **ex-convent** attached to the church houses the **Museum of Oaxacan Cultures** (10 am to 6 pm, closed Mondays, 516 2991). It traces Oaxaca's roots from prehispanic times through the conquest and on to today's multicultural mix. Make sure to visit Room III, which displays the intricate golden treasures from Monte Albán's Tomb 7. **Visit the museum early in your stay.** It will deepen your appreciation of the city, the surrounding *pueblos*, and archaeological sites. The displays don't have English explanations, making the **audioguide** worthwhile.

From the museum, you will be able to glimpse the **Ethnobotanic Gardens.** We highly recommend a visit. The gardens feature an extensive collection of cacti and other regional plants utilized by *Oaxaqueños* past and present, in a beautiful setting. Visitors are not allowed to tour the gardens on their own, so sign up in advance for tours in English, currently scheduled for Tuesday, Thursday and Saturday at 11 am, for $100 pesos. If your Spanish is good, you can take the shorter but more frequent tours in Spanish for $50 pesos. **The schedule changes frequently, so check in advance..** Drop by the entrance at the corner of Reforma and Constitución, or phone 516 5325 to sign up. There's not much shade, so bring water and a hat.

The **Basílica de Nuestra Señora de la Soledad** is not to be missed. The façade features a beautiful bas-relief of Mary as the grieving mother. The ornate altar displays a dazzling statue of the Virgin of Solitude graced with a jewel-laden gold crown. Soledad's **museum** features stained-glass panels depicting the miraculous appearance of images of Jesus and the Virgin in 1620.

The broad steps adjoining Soledad are full of stands offering aM variety of goods, including **handmade ices and ice creams**. Friends tell us that the *tamarindo* (tamarind) at Niagra is the best. The place we prefer for traditional Oaxacan ice cream is **Manolo Nieves** at its new outlet at Alcala # 707. Try the *cacahuate*.

For those wanting to explore Oaxaca's history in more depth, artist **Linda Martín** leads walking tours of several colonial churches, starting in front of the Cathedral at 10am on Tuesday and Saturday. She has a wealth of information to share. You can just show up, but It's better to contact her in advance at ridgecliff@hotmail.com. Linda suggests a donation of $100 pesos per person, all of which goes to charity.

The recently restored **Casa de la Ciudad** at Porfirio Díaz 115, at the corner of Morelos, merits a visit (free, open every day from 9am to 8pm). It's a classic colonial building redone by the same architect who so beautifully restored Santo Domingo. Here the result is elegant and understated. Exhibits dealing with the present city and its history and architecture change frequently. The Andrés Henestrosa Library houses 40,000 volumes on art, architecture, and Latin American history and literature.

The nearby **Museo Rufino Tamayo**, at Morelos 503, houses the famed artist's personal collection of prehispanic, colonial and modern art and artifacts. It's open Monday plus Wednesday through Saturday from 10 am to 2 pm and 4 pm to 7 pm; on Sundays from 10 am to 3 pm, closed Tuesdays. If you call at 516 4750, they may be able to schedule a docent tour in English. If not, the displays are described in English, Spanish and French.

Museo Textil de Oaxaca–Textile Museum of Oaxaca: If you're interested in weavers and weaving from around the world, this new museum in a beautifully redone colonial building at the corner of Hidalgo and Fiallo in the center of Oaxaca is well worth a visit. We've seen several impressive shows there. The museum also sponsors a variety of programs and hands-on workshops. Open from 10 am to 8 pm daily except for Tuesday. Entry is free. (Tel: (951) 501 1104; www.museotextildeoaxaca.org.mx.)

Museum Belber Jimenez: Federico and Ellen Belber Jimenez have opened a museum with the theme of **design in Mexico** to complement their store, Federico's, at the corner of Matamoros and Tinoco y Palacios. The small musuem is well worth a visit. It features outstanding handcrafted jewelry, works in silver, *tapetes*, embroidered goods, and ceramics in the rooms of a beautifully restored colonial building, around a classic courtyard. (www.museobelberjimenez.org/; Tel: 514 5095).

Art and photography lovers should also check out the **Museum of Contemporary Art** (MACO) at Alcalá 202, open from 10:30 am to 8 pm; the **Institute of Graphic Arts** at Alcalá 507, 9:30 am to 8 pm; and the **Centro Fotografico Alvarez Bravo** at M. Bravo 116, open from 9:30 am to 8 pm with its frequently changing and sometimes striking photography exhibits (all closed on Tuesdays).

It's worth dropping by the main **Library of Oaxaca**, at Alcalá 200. The inner patios of this 300-year-old building are enchanting. As a bonus, you can **check your email for free** at the back of the second patio. (Monday through Friday 9 am to 8:30 pm, Saturday 9 am to 2 pm, closed Sunday).

The grand old **Teatro Macedonio Alcalá** (corner of Cinco de Mayo and Independencia) reopened in 2004 after six years of restoration. Its multi-tiered white and gold concert hall is the perfect setting for Oaxaca's best music, dance and theater.

Teatro Macedonio Alcalá

It's well worth catching an event there, if only to enjoy the interior of the theater. Special exhibits are sometimes held on the upper floor of the building, accessed via an ornately carved wooden staircase. Look for the open doorway on Independencia, to the left of the main entrance, where you can check the schedule and purchase tickets.

Mexico's only indigenous president, the revered **Benito Juárez**, was from Oaxaca, and his **former home** at García Vigil 609 is now a lovingly restored museum (closed Mondays).

Near the zócalo, at the corner of Independencia and Garcia Vigil, across from the Alameda de León park, is the **Museo de Pintores Oaxaqueños** (Museum of Oaxacan Painters). The colonial beauty of the building serves as a fitting backdrop to exhibits featuring the work of such famed local artists as Rodolfo Morales and Rufino Tamayo as well as lesser known artists. Tuesday to Saturday from 10 am to 8 pm; closed Monday; entry $20 pesos.

Benito Juarez dominates a mural in the new Museo del Palacio

On the west side of the zócalo, the former *Palacio de Gobierno* (site of state government) has been converted into the **Museo del**

Palacio (10 am to 6 pm daily, closed Monday). The spacious colonial edifice houses a pair of vivid murals by Arturo Garcia Bustos, a disciple of Frida Kahlo, depicting the history of Oaxaca, plus changing exhibits and events dealing with Oaxaca's history, culture, art and architecture. Their Day of the Dead exhibits are usually striking. **Note::** don't be too shocked if you can't get in because demonstrators have blocked the entrance!

Be sure to dive into the ever-lively **covered markets, Benito Juárez** and **20 de Noviembre**, both just south of the *zócalo*, and the **Artisans' Market** on J.P. García between Mina and Zaragoza. Near the markets, follow your nose to the factories on Mina grinding Oaxaca's famous **chocolate** by the shovelful. It's a great show, and most of the shops offer free tastes. See which mixture of fresh cocoa, cinnamon, almonds, and sugar you like best.

Basket vendors at the entrance to Oaxaca's covered market

On Fridays, a busy outdoor market takes place in Llano Park (officially known as *Parque Juarez*), just south of the Guadalupe church and bordered by Avenida Juarez and Calle Pino Suarez. This is a good place to buy fresh fruits and vegetables, meat, fish, beauty items, CDs and DVDs, jewelry, clothing, and almost anything else you can think of. There are also lots of stands selling freshly prepared food to eat on site or take away. Follow your nose, and see where most people are congregated.

A small but high-quality organic market takes place on Friday and Saturday from 8 am to 4 pm in the churchyard of Xochimilco, the neighborhood just north of the center of town. Go up Porfirio Díaz, cross Niños Heroes, climb the stairs, and continue one block farther north.

Out and about

Monte Albán is the star attraction outside Oaxaca (open daily 8 am to 5 pm). It occupies a flattened hilltop overlooking the city. The reconstructed ruins of this great Zapotec ceremonial center--said to be the first urban center in mesoamerica, with a peak population of 25,000--are impressive, mysterious and photogenic. We were particularly intrigued by arrow-shaped "**Building J,**" thought to be an observatory. There is only one similar building in all of ancient mesoamerica, at Caballito Blanco about 30 miles east of Monte Albán. You can read more about the ancient astronomers of Monte Albán on our website, www.si-oaxaca.com/a_bit_of_archaeoastronomy.htm.

Try to get to Monte Albán as early in the morning as possible, when the light is best . Bring a hat, sunblock, and plenty of water! If you can, climb the south platform for the view. We suggest touring the excellent on-site museum first. Hiring one of the licensed guides at the site can add a lot to your visit. We highly recommend **Juan Adalberto Lopez Ramos.** You may find him at the site, or contact him in advance at (951) 547 1947 or adalbertguia@hotmail.com.

Archaeologists tell us that the complex was started around 500 BC and was occupied for nearly fourteen centures. They haven't been able to decipher its hieroglyphics, apart from names and numbers, nor determine why the site was abandoned around 850 AD. Nor have experts agreed on an explanation for **Los Danzantes**, a collection of striking carved figures including hunchbacks, dwarves, and mutilated people. Were they captive chiefs, as many archaeologists think? Medical case studies? What's your theory?

Mysterious Building J at Monte Albán

East of Oaxaca lies **Mitla**, a major city that was founded more than 1000 years later than Monte Albán. Its mixed Zapotec-Mixtec architecture is totally different from Monte Albán's — far less massive, and decorated with exquisite, intriguing "greca" fretwork. Unlike Monte Albán, Mitla was still occupied when the *conquistadores* arrived. As was their custom, the conquerors planted their churches on top of earlier buildings. The current town overlies the ancient city, only tantalizing parts of which have been excavated. If your Spanish is good, look for **Bonifacio Bautista Aragon,** an excellent licensed guide to the ruins.

Independent travelers should note that some second-class buses from Oaxaca to Mitla drop passengers off along the main highway, a mile or so from the ruins and the **San Pablo Apostol Church** (also worth visiting). Make sure that your bus or *colectivo* will take you to the the very center of the town--*"al mero centro de Mitla"* – or be prepared for a hike.

Another popular tourist destination, **Hierve el Agua**, is in the hill country east of Mitla. You've almost certainly seen pictures of its gleaming white cliffs. It's worth a visit, particularly if you like hiking. During or soon after the rainy season, you might enjoy a refreshing dip in a natural pool with truly spectacular views.

Tours to Mitla usually stop at **Santa María el Tule**, a small town with a giant tree more than 160 feet in diameter and 2000 years old. It's said to be the most massive tree in the world, although not the tallest or oldest. On Sundays, the same tour also takes you to **Tlacolula** for its **weekly market**, and a chance to admire its beautiful church and glittering, sculpture-filled chapel.

Four kilometers north of El Tule, near San Andrés Huayapam, liesT the little-known **La Encantada Orquideario**, a magical orchid preserve created by architect Octavio Gabriel Suárez. In theory, La Encantada is open daily from 10am to 5pm. However, since Sr. Suárez runs La Encantada on a shoestring, and leads most tours himself, it's best to contact him in advance for times and detailed directions (Email: oencantada@hotmail.com; cellphone 044 951 119 4214, www.epulinc.com/orquideario/index.htm). There's a map on the website – click on *Ubicacion*. You're more likely to find Sr. Suarez at the *orquideario* on the weekend.

To Teotitlán del Valle and beyond

East of El Tule you'll find **Teotitlán del Valle**, world-famous for its *tapetes* – hand-woven wool rugs. In Teotitlán nearly every house is a *taller* (workshop), ranging from large and tourist-oriented to tiny and humble. We like wandering from house to house to check outB the small family operations.

Tours from Oaxaca generally take you to only one rug-weaving establishment. To see more, visit Teotitlán on your own, or you can make arrangements with Tapetes de Oaxaca ar 515-5707. Roger, a native English speaker, will take you to a variety of workshops. Many of the larger weaving workshops will offer to show you how wool is carded, spun, dyed (in most cases with vegetable or other natural dyes) and woven. It's a fascinating process.

Internationally known **Arnulfo Mendoza** is arguably the most famous weaver in Teotitlán del Valle. You can see his exquisite creations at his workshop along the main road at kilometer 4. Another well-known *taller* in Teotitlán is that of **Isaac Vasquez**, called the **Bug in the Rug**, at Hidalgo 30. His designs are quite different from Sr. Mendoza's, and to some even more appealing.

Just around the corner at Iturbide # 32, the **Centro de Arte Textil Zapoteco Bii Daüü**, an innovative indigenous weaving co-op, merits a visit. Be sure to check out their upstairs loft.

You'll also find a showroom full ofBii superb *tapetes* at **Casa Cruz,** owned by Fidel Cruz Lazo and María Luisa Mendoza Ruiz, at Avenida Juárez, kilometer 2, on the road's east side.

Pastora Gutiérrez Reyes of "Vida Nueva"

Also at kilometer 2, **El Encanto,** run by weaver Pantaleon Ruiz Martinez and extended family, offers beautiful tapetes of pure wool and natural colors. Our friends have come back with lovely new rugs from there or from the Martinez home at Hidalgo 46 in Teotitlán.

A family *taller* well worth visiting is **Manos Que Tejen,**, Hands that Weave, at Avenida Juarez # 109. Their incorporation of modern designs into a traditional art form has produced beautiful results.

The *taller* of **Josefina Mendez Lopez**, at Guerrero # 9 in Teotitlán, has many beautiful and well woven *tapetes* on display, made of 100% pure wool and natural dyes. They also will be happy to take you through the carding, dyeing and weaving process. Cell: 044 951 151 1395.

We also suggest a visit to the family of **Federico Chavez**, at Francisco Madero # 55 in Teotitlán. This is a lovely and accomplished family making fine tapetes using authentic natural dyes. They also have a a small shop in Oaxaca at 5 de Mayo # 408, Interior # 1.

Past Teotitlan's open-air crafts market and the *Palacio Municipal*, you'll find a street heading down and to the right. The first gate on the left, marked Centenario #1, leads to **Vida Nueva**, a Zapotec women's weaving co-op (and multi-function women's center). They have lots of beautiful rugs on display, incorporating prehispanic, traditional, and original designs.

If you would like a *tapete* made to order, you can get a beautiful and well-woven rug at a fair price from the small workshop of **Joel Gonzalez** and his son **Eden** at Avenida Juarez # 43. You can see their work at www.si-oaxaca.com/Joel_and_Eden_Gonzalez.htm. Design your own rug or select from traditional designs, pick the size and colors you want, and it will be woven and shipped to you.

Remember that bargaining is acceptable at all of Teotitlán's *tapete* outlets, especially if you are buying more than one rug.

We like to finish a visit to Teotitlán with a leisurely afternoon meal of traditional Zapotec food at **Tlamanalli** (Juárez 39, open from 1:15pm to 4pm). See "**Where to eat**" below for details.

Santa Ana del Valle–the other rug-weaving town: is just off the beaten track. You get to Santa Ana along route 190 that heads east from Oaxaca past El Tule, the **ruins of Dainzu', Lambityeco, and Yagul** (all worth visiting), and on to Mitla. Turn north at Tlacolula on the road towards Díaz Ordaz, and follow signs to the center of Santa Ana, just minutes from the highway. In addition to a small market displaying traditional *tapetes*, many made with natural colors, you'll also find a small but interesting museum dedicated to the town's history and prehistory, a beautiful 16th-century church, and a tiny church museum. You may need to ask the person in charge of the town museum to unlock the church and let you in.

South of Oaxaca

Friday is the day to take a tour south to catch **Ocotlan's colorful market day**, or tianguis. Go early in the day to see Zapotec men, women and children selling hats, pottery, fruits, vegetables (including heaps of *chiles*), herbs, spices, *copal* (a traditional incense made from the sap of a local tree), and even goats and turkeys. The raised area of the bandstand in the middle of the square has a very nice selection of handicrafts, including painted gourds, woven items, knives, blouses and dresses, *alebrijes* (the fanciful carved and painted animals for which Oaxaca is famous), and much more.

Tianguis--market day

Don't miss Ocotlan's ornate 16-th Century church, with its blue,white and yellow façade, restored by the beloved local artist **Rudolfo Morales** (1925-2001). As you leave the church, turn right, go through the gate, and find the **museum** at the corner. It contains lovely photographs of and works by Morales, truly a man of the people. (The museum also has a cafeteria and the nicest bathrooms in town!) Upstairs in the museum is a collection of enchanting, often hilarious ceramic figures by the famous **Aguilar family**, whose work is featured in various books on Oaxacan crafts. You can visit their workshops along the road back toward Oaxaca (Prolongacíon de Morelos, no number).

You can see more of Morales' art in Oaxaca at **Arte de Oaxaca gallery**, Murguia 105, and in the **Museum of Oaxacan Painters..**

The popularity of Ocotlan's market has attracted pickpockets. Stay alert and avoid getting hemmed in by a crowd of people.

About 30 km south of Ocotlán lies the town of **Ejutla de Crespo**. We love their **weekly market, on Thursday**. Very few tourists make it out there, so the *tianguis* is particularly authentic and colorful.

Mermaid and Neptune ceramic at the Ocotlán museum

For artistic, attractive and useable crafts, stop in the town of **Santo Tomás Jalieza**, known for the intricately patterned cotton textiles — purses, table runners, placemats, and much more— woven on backstrap looms by local women and girls. Santo Tomás Jalieza maintains a pleasant outdoor cooperative market where you'll find lots of handwoven items to choose from.

A bit closer to Oaxaca you'll find **San Martin Tilcajete**, where a visit to the home and workshop of master woodcarvers **Jacobo and Maria Angeles Ojeda** is a must. You can preview their carvings at www.tilcajete.org/, see some examples at their restaurant, **Azucena Zapoteca**, at the turnoff from the main road to the pueblo, or meet them and watch their extended family at work at their studio on Calle Olvido # 9, in San Martin. Jacobo's exquisite work more than justifies his worldwide renown.

Even closer to Oaxaca lies the village of **San Bartolo Coyotepec**, known for its gleaming black ceramics. Don't miss the lovely **Museo Estatal de Arte Popular** (State Museum of Popular Art), located on the main square next door to the *Palacio Municipal*. On display are some of the most stunning ceramic art and wood carvings we've seen. There's a vivid preview at: http://www.aquioaxaca.com/museos/artepopular_museo.htm. The musem has an excellent shop (open 10am to 6pm, closed Mondays, 551 0036), and the town has many places to shop for black pottery.

Detail from a piece in Coyotepec's State Museum of Popular Art

Southwest of Oaxaca

Thursday is the best day to head southwest of Oaxaca, for the **market day of Zaachila** plus stops in **Cuilápan and San Antonio Arrazola**.. Zaachila's outdoor market is one of the best we've seen. It has an amazing assortment of goods, few of which are aimed at tourists. You won't see a lot of crafts, but you will see live turkeys, all kinds of fruits and vegetables, delicious food including *barbacoa de ricos pollos* (savory barbecued chicken), shoes, CD's, kitchen items, blue jeans, spices, hats, flowers, furniture, baskets, and much more.

Across from the market you'll see the colorfully painted, multi-domed church. Just around the corner and uphill from the church, a flight of stairs will lead you to **Zaachila's small archaeological site.** Although Zaachila is known as the cradle of the Zapotec empire, only a corner of the ruins that underlie today's town has been excavated. On the left you'll see a dusty hill that hides an unexcavated temple. It's worth climbing to the top for the view and the sense of standing atop an undisturbed bit of prehistory.

The lower part of the site consists of a plaza containing two tombs. Ask at the ticket booth for the lights to be turned on so you can **descend into the tombs to see the striking bas-reliefs of owl-gods and human-turtle and human–serpent chimeras.** Also ask to see the photo album of artifacts taken from the tombs.

On the outskirts of Zaachila you can stop for good, albeit expensive, *comida tipica* at **La Capilla** (see **"Where to eat"** section for details). It's a great place to try *tacos con chapulines* (grasshopper tacos)!

Never-finished convent at Cuilápan

On the way back to Oaxaca you can wander the ruins of the huge, fascinating, never-completed **convent at Cuilápan de Guerrero..** And just off the highway lies tiny **Arrazola,**, a town famous for its fanciful carved wooden *alebrijes*. As in Teotitlán, nearly every house is also a workshop and salesroom. Bargaining is expected.

Northwest of Oaxaca

Art lovers should not miss **CASA, Centro de las Artes de San Agustín,** located in San Agustín, Etla (www.casanagustin.org, 521 3042, 521 3043 or 521 2574, 9am to 6pm daily). Walk past the church and across the plaza at the top of Av. Independencia to reach the center. Appropriately called **Vista Hermosa**—beautiful view--the center occupies a huge refurbished cloth factory built in 1883. CASA usually features a worthwhile exhibit — we just saw an exposition of superb ceramics—plus concerts and artistic activities. It's worth the 10-mile *colectivo*, taxi or car ride just to tour the site, even if there isn't an exhibit in progress. (Be sure to climb the spiral staircase to the giant upstairs space and front and rear terraces, and Jo Ann suggests that you take a look at the ladies' room.) Up steps from the table where you check in lies the *Taller de Arte Papel--* the art paper worksho*p,* where you can buy unique handmade paper kites, earrings and other jewelry.

Farther north along Route 190, **La Ruta Dominicana,** lies a series of impressive Dominican churches and convents built soon after the Spanish conquest of Mexico. Three well worth visiting are in Yanhuitlán, Coixtlhuaca, and San Pedro y San Pablo Teposcolula. These can be seen on a long day trip from Oaxaca, although we recommend setting out as early in the day as possible. Sunday is not the best day to go since the churches will be closed.

Where to stay

Oaxaca is full of great hotel choices. There are charming bed and breakfasts, lavish colonial hotels, upscale modern-ish hotels, and hotels for every budget. **The rates shown below are in US dollars for a standard double room in high season, including the mandatory 18% tax.** Since hotels frequently offer special rates, we recommend checking current prices and making sure that the price you are quoted includes the 18% tax.

As an alternative to a hotel, you can stay at one of Oaxaca's many lovely B &B's. You will find a **list of quality B & Bs and small hotels,** with links, at www.oaxacabedandbreakfast.org/, the website for Oaxaca's Bed and Breakfast Association. Among the many fine offerings are long-time favorites like the beautiful **Casa Colonial** (http://www.casa-colonial.com/), and newer options like **Casa Machaya** (http://www.oaxacadream.com/), **Casa Adobe** (http://www.casaadobe-bandb.com/), and **Oaxaca Ollin** (http://www.oaxacabedandbreakfast.com/).

You can see **visitors' ratings and comments** about hotels and B&Bs in Oaxaca at: http://www.tripadvisor.com/Hotels-g150801-Oaxaca_Pacific_Coast-Hotels.html.

To call a number in Oaxaca from the U.S. or Canada, dial your international access code, followed by Mexico's country code, **52**, then Oaxaca's area code, **951**, followed by the rest of the number. To make a local call from Oaxaca, all you will need to dial is the seven-digit local number. If you're calling a Oaxaca cell phone from a landline in Oaxaca, you will have to dial **044 951** and then the seven-digit number.

Very Expensive ($141 to $350 per night)

The pre-eminent hotel in town is **El Camino Real Oaxaca**, at Cinco de Mayo 300, in the 400 year old **ex-convent of Santa Catalina**.. The Camino Real is as colonial as they come, with gorgeous courtyards, lovely gardens, and mysterious corridors, yet with a modern swimming pool. In the back corner of the grounds you can still see the beautiful fountain where the nuns did their laundry. The 91 rooms, while nicely decorated with warm colors and high-quality furnishings, are somewhat small and, depending on location, can be noisy. (516 0611; free from the U.S. (800) 722-6466 or 901-2300; www.camino-real-oaxaca.com)

Our favorite 5-star choice is **Posada Casa Oaxaca,** García Vigil 407, at the other end of the style spectrum from El Camino Real. It is simple and elegant, even somewhat spare. It, too, is built around an open courtyard, and has a lovely swimming pool. The interior of the hotel's public areas is painted white, and its seven rooms are large and feel cool. Casa Oaxaca is also distinguished by its extremely helpful staff and the quality of its on-site kitchen. Guests tell us that they look forward to getting up every morning just to enjoy the fabulous breakfast! Free internet access. Rates are lower than El Camino Real, and include breakfast. (www.casaoaxaca.com; (514-4173).

The **Hotel de la Parra**, a few blocks from the *zócalo* at Guerrero 117, has just 10 rooms and suites and an extremely

One of the Camino Real's courtyards

friendly, helpful staff. Its public spaces include a pleasant garden and small swimming pool. (Phone:5141900; www.hoteldelaparra.net).

For something a little removed from the hustle and bustle of the center of town, the 1950-ish **Hotel Victoria** is an attractive alternative. Built on a hill overlooking Oaxaca at Carretera Internacional km. 545, the Victoria has been re-decorated for current tastes. It features cottages set out amidst the hotel's gardens, and a lovely swimming pool. The terrace bar, with its great view, is a relaxing place to savor the end of the day. (515 2633; www.hotelvictoriaoax.com.mx)

Expensive ($101 to $140 per night)

The **Casa de Sierra Azul** at Hidalgo 1002 is in a converted 19th century mansion near the *zócalo*. Its fifteen rooms are very large and surround a spacious patio enhanced by a fountain in the center. (514 7171; www.hotelcasadesierrazul.com)

The relatively new **Casa Catrina**, at García Vigil 703, was designed by its young owner, architect and painter Rolando Rojas. Its six extremely comfortable, large and well-appointed rooms surround a central courtyard. Rojas' impressive paintings hang in each room, and his architectural and decorative touches create a zen-like elegance. On-site temazcal. Rates include a Oaxacan-style breakfast. (516 0519; www.casacatrina.com.mx)

At the north end of town, near Conzatti and Llano parks, is the cheerful **Casa Conzatti Hotel**, at Gómez Farías 218. Its 45 rooms, pleasant open areas and café make this a good choice if you'd prefer a quieter location slightly further from the center of town. (513 8500; www.oaxacalive.com/conzatti/). Ask if they're offering any promotional rates.

The **Hotel Parador San Miguel**, Av. Independencia 503, is conveniently located two blocks west of the *zócalo*. Its 19 pleasant double rooms and four nicely decorated suites (with jacuzzis) feature air conditioning, cable TV, plus some facilities for guests with disabilities. Rates vary by season. (514 9331; www.mexonline.com/paradorsanmiguel.htm)

An excellent choice is the **Hostal Casa del Sótano**, at Tinoco y Palacios 414. We've sent many friends and family members there. The former home of the Sótano family, the hotel has 23 colonial-style rooms and a suite. Built around an attractive interior courtyard, the hotel has extremely helpful staff and lovely views of Santo Domingo church from its roof garden and breakfast area. (516 2494; http://www.hoteldelsotano.net/)

If you like being in *el mero centro*, right in the middle of things, you'll enjoy the gracious **Hotel Marqués del Valle**, with its incomparable location on the north side of the zócalo. There are several types of rooms, some recently remodeled, some with air conditioning, others with fans, some in the interior of the building, and many with great views. (514 0688 or 516 3474; www.hotelmarquesdelvalle.com.mx)

Moderate ($71 to $100 per night)

The **Hotel Aitana**, at Crespo 313, has 23 rooms in a remodeled

16th century colonial home. Breakfast is served in an interior patio, and the sun terrace has a lovely view of the city. (514 3788, 514 3839; www.hotelaitanaoaxaca.com.mx)

The newish **Hotel Casa Vertiz**, Reforma 404, is close to Santo Domingo church and offers 14 rooms with air conditioning, telephones, and internet. It has an attractive patio restaurant and rooftop terrace. (516 2525; www.hotelvertiz.com.mx)

A boutique hotel near the Ethnobotanic Garden at Constitución 203, the **Casa de los Frailes** has 10 nicely decorated rooms and a peaceful feeling. Double rooms feature 2 standard double beds; larger beds available. Rates include continental breakfast (514 1151; www.casadelosfrailes.com)

Casa de las Bugambilias B and B is located at Reforma 402, behind La Olla restaurant. Las Bugambilias provides a quiet retreat, generous breakfasts, and large rooms and public areas decorated with museum-quality pieces of folk art. Low-cost international phone calls are also available. (516 1165; toll free from the U.S., (877) OAX CASA; www.lasbugambilias.com)

Budget ($41 to $70 per night)

Our favorite B & B is **Hotel Las Mariposas**, at Pino Suárez 517. Rooms are nicely decorated, and there are two lovely patios for relaxing, including one where a family-style continental breakfast is provided and guests congregate. (Note: breakfast is light, just coffee or tea, cereal, and a selection of bread). Multi-talented owner Teresa Villarreal and her daughter Lucía are some of the most helpful and well-informed contacts you could have in Oaxaca. Las Mariposas is just a couple of blocks from Santo Domingo church and is close to Llano Park, one of the prettiest spots in town. Free internet access is provided, including wireless. There's also a shared patio kitchen and wine bar, plus a TV lounge. Guests can make low-cost phone calls to the U.S. and Canada and free calls to anywhere in Mexico. Rooms with kitchenettes are also available. (515 5854; from the U.S. and Canada, (619) 793-5121; www.lasmariposas.com.mx)

Another perennial favorite in the budget range is **Hotel Las**

Golondrinas, at Tinoco y Palacios 411. The hotel is on a noisy street, but the lush gardens help block out traffic sounds. To be on the safe side, ask for an interior room. The rooms, while simple, are large and clean. This is a place where guests return year after year, despite complaints about inflexibility on the part of management. Breakfast is not included. (514 2095; www.hotellasgolondrinas.com.mx)

Hotel Azucenas is located at Prof. M. Aranda 203, at Matamoros —a slightly out of the way corner that looks like the cobblestoned street of a village, but in reality is only a block away from Soledad Basilica and five blocks from the *zócalo*. Set in a restored colonial home, the rooms are comfortable and the view from the garden terrace is unforgettable. Rates include coffee all day. Breakfast is an extra $44 pesos. (514 7918; toll free from the U.S., (877) 780-1156; www.hotelazucenas.com)

You can enjoy a centrally located B&B, and help support a worthy program, by staying at **The Learning Center**, Murguia 703. Its owner, Gary Titus, uses the proceeds from his comfortable and well-equipped rooms and spacious two-room apartment to help young men and women from outlying *pueblos* with personalized guidance and tutoring, support for their education, and job training. (515 0122; www.learningcenteroaxaca.com)

If you are seriously interested in **Oaxacan crafts and folk art**, consider staying at **Casa Linda**, located in the quiet town of Huayapam, a short car or bus ride outside Oaxaca. The B & B is in a magical setting and is brimming with beautifully displayed folk art and fine art. The owner, Linda Hanna, is an expert who knows most of the region's artisans personally, and will be happy to take you out to meet them. (540 8020; www.folkartfantasy.com)

For a restful stay from a few days to a month in a lovely setting, consider **La Casa de los Abuelos**, centrally located at Reforma # 410. The owner, charming and efficient Rosita, offers 8 comfortable suites, some with king sized beds, some with queens, and some with the slightly smaller *matrimonial* beds. All rooms have TV, internet, refrigerator and coffeemaker. Breakfast is not included. The house itself is a 200-year-old colonial style building surrounding a charming and tranquil inner courtyard. It's the sort of place that visitors come back to year after year. Prices start at $60 US per night for two people, with a reduction for longer stays. (Telephone: 516 1982; www.lacasa-de-rosita.com; email: lacasadelosabuelos@hotmail.com)

Hotel Aurora, at Bustamonte 212, emerges as a good option for a comfortable, centrally located hotel in the lower price range. Their 32 rooms are pleasant and clean and have modern bathrooms. Wireless internet in the hotel lobby. The hotel is very close to the zócalo and downtown covered markets. (516 3447 or 516 4145, www.hotelauroraoaxaca.com; hotel-aurora@hotmail.com)

Where to eat in and around Oaxaca

Oaxacan cuisine is justifiably famous. Like the historic center, Oaxacan cuisine has been designated by UNESCO as part of the World Heritage, "A Masterpiece of the Oral and Intangible Heritage of Humanity."

In addition to dishes that you can find in Mexican restaurants anywhere in the world, specialties typical of Oaxaca include its seven different kinds of *moles* (pronounced MOH-lays), of which *mole negro* and *mole rojo* (black *mole* and red *mole*, usually served over chicken or as a filling for tortillas) are the richest and most complex; *tlayudas*, large crispy tortillas topped with a variety of ingredients to make a pizza-like dish; *tamales* with various fillings, of which those wrapped in banana leaves and stuffed with black *mole* are the most typical; and a range of excellent soups.

Oaxacans cook with some herbs that are little known elsewhere. If you have a taste for something different, try dishes featuring **hierba santa** or **hoja santa**, a large leaf with a unique licorice-like flavor; **huitlacoche**, a black fungus that grows on corn and is sometimes characterized as Mexico's truffle; **epazote**, a small leafy herb with a spinach-like flavor, often used in *quesadillas*; or **chepil**, used in soups, stews, tamales and rice.

Try to get in synch with local eating hours: a small breakfast; **almuerzo** around 11:00; **comida**, the largest meal, starting around 3:00; and, if you have room, a lighter **cena** sometime after 8:00. Because, by local mores, it would be impolite to bring your bill before being asked for it, you'll always need to request it — "*La cuenta, por favor.*" To get your waiter's attention, you can call "*Joven*" (young man) or "*señorita* (young lady). A downward wave of the hand is a polite way to signal "come here."

Restaurants serving tourists use purified water for ice and drinks, and carefully disinfect fruits and vegetables. Although *chiles* are used in many dishes, we have rarely found the food too *picante*, but if you're worried, you can ask how spicy the food will be ("*¿Pica mucho?*"), or request "*No muy picante, por favor.*"

Please note that Oaxaca's restaurants often change their schedules without notice. If you want to be sure of having a meal in a particular place, it's best to call in advance to make sure that the restaurant will be open when you want to go.

For consumer ratings and reviews of restaurants, click on www.pruebalo.com.mx/ranking.php. For unknown reasons, these recommendations seem to us to favor Italian, seafood, and other restaurants featuring non-Oaxacan cuisine. Don't miss out on Oaxaca's superb local/typical cuisine!

How well done do your want your meat?

The very thin cuts that go into many Oaxacan dishes, such as *tlayudas*, will usually be well done. But if you order a steak or other thick cut of meat, you may be asked or want to specify how well done you'd like it.

In Spanish, the crucial word is *termino* (done). For example, a waiter may ask, "*¿Que termino quiere?*" The following terms should work in most restaurants: *termino ingles* or *termino rojo ingles*—extremely rare; *termino rojo*—rare; *termino medio rojo*—medium rare; *termino medio*—medium; *termino tres quartos*—well done; *termino bien cocido*—very well done.

Fine dining

Our first choice for a special meal is the restaurant **Casa Oaxaca (Constitución 104-A, very expensive, reservations recommended, 516 8889)**,, related to but not the same as the hotel by the same name. Their eclectic and sophisticated menu changes frequently, but you can always get an elegant version of a traditional Oaxacan *mole*. Their soups, salads and appetizers are superb. Anything you order will be delicious, and beautifully presented. Like the courtyard of its sister hotel, **Posada Casa Oaxaca**, the restaurant's dining patio is a study in elegant simplicity. The staff clearly have been well trained by congenial, talented, and renowned executive chef and general manager Alejandro Ruiz. The comfortable bar now features delicious *tentenpies*, small tapas-style dishes. Open 1pm to 11pm daily, 11 to 9 on Sunday. Their downstairs bar and rooftop terrace are delightful places to relax.

A well-kept secret: For a superb, if a bit pricey, breakfast in one of the most elegant patios in Oaxaca, ring the doorbell outside the discretely closed doors of the hotel **Casa Oaxaca** (Garcia Vigil 417) any morning. You'll be rewarded with delicious American or Oaxacan food and attentive service in a tranquil setting. Calling ahead, if not a hotel guest, is appreciated.

The elegant restaurant in the courtyard of the Hotel Casa Oaxaca is **also available for *comida* or *cena*.** Spurred by a French friend who was dying to check out their food, drink and *ambiente*, we had a superb meal there. The diners were given personalized service by the chef, who came out to show us their fresh fish and giant shrimp. Following his suggestion, our table sampled red snapper prepared in three different ways, plus the shrimp, all of which were delicious. Their meat dishes and Oaxacan specialties are also first rate. We had a great dining experience. Highly recommended for a somewhat expensive, but very special night out. **Reservations required.** Tel: 951 516 9923 or 951 514 4173.

Another lovely spot for a special breakfast is the **Hotel Victoria**, on a hill above Oaxaca. They offer an excellent buffet from 7 am to noon every day. Currently $150 pesos per person.

The other "top" restaurant in Oaxaca is **Los Danzantes** (Alcalá 403-4, expensive, 501 1184 or 1187, 1:30 pm to midnight daily). It offers a striking *ambiente* and one of the best bars in Oaxaca. We and friends think their food is excellent, if a bit pricey. It's worth stopping by or calling to see if they are offering their *comida corrida* (starting around 1:30 pm Wednesdays and Fridays). The price is 95 pesos, higher than our usual cut-off for *comida corrida*, but given the hiqh quality of their offerings, it's a good deal.

For a fabulous steak, we recommend **El Ché,** an Argentine-style restaurant (corner of Belisario Dominguez and Amapolas in Colonia Reforma, expensive, reservations recommended, 515 1999). They're open from 1:30pm to 11pm Monday through Saturday, 1:30pm to 9:00pm Sunday. **El Ché has closed its branch in the center of Oaxaca and has opened a new site, Che Gaucho, at Las Rosas #700 (corner of Alamos, 514 2122) also in Colonia Reforma.** Meat lovers will find this a real treat.

La Biznaga (García Vigil 512, between Allende and Carranza, moderately expensive, 516 1800) remains our favorite place for afternoon *comida* or evening *cena,* and continues to delight us and the many friends we bring there. Open from 1pm to 10pm Monday through Thursday, 1pm through 11pm on Friday and Saturday, closed on Sunday.

Run by talented Mexico-city-trained chef Fernando López and his brother Nacho, La Biznaga features the freshest of local and organic ingredients combined in surprising and delicious ways. We think of it as *nueva cocina Mexicana*--nouvelle cuisine, Mexican style. It also has an excellent bar that features a selection of fine beers, including great house-made brews, plus refreshing, lightly fermented *pulque* (agave juice), and makes absolutely **dynamite margaritas** –the best in town.

To start, try the *tamalitos de hierba santa*, local cheese melted with *flor de calabaza* inside the leaf of a slightly licorice-flavored herb; or the *sopa seca de fideos con chorizo*, fine pasta and sausage in a spicy sauce; or share an ample salad. Then have *pollo relleno de rajas y flor de calabaza*, chicken flavored with squash blossoms and strips of chili; or chicken accompanied by *platanos machos*, plantains in a guava-flavored sauce; or *mole negro* with mushrooms and an inspired touch of blackberries; or beef smothered in a sauce of *chile*, prunes and *mezcal*. Their salmon with cilantro pesto is also a knockout.

Noted local architect Viviana Ruiz designed La Biznaga's spacious patio with just enough artistic touches to make it interesting, shaded by a movable canvas ceiling high overhead. Since both brothers are musicians, the background music they choose is varied and interesting, although some find it too loud. Fernando prides himself on making everything to order, so **be prepared to spend at least a couple of hours savoring the "slow food."**

Chef Fernando López lists La Biznaga's specials

Another place for fine and interesting dining is **Meson del Olivo** at Murguia # 218 (corner of Reforma) in the historic center, offering succulent **Spanish** and Oaxacan dishes. We wolfed down an appetizer of sauteed *setas* (a particularly tasty kind of mushroom), loved their spinach soup, onion soup and garlic soup, and thoroughly enjoyed one of their signature dishes, *codornices* (quail) with fine herbs. Their meat dishes are succulent. The spacious downstairs restaurant is open from around 1 pm to midnight daily., and the upstairs *tapas* bar from around 4 p.m. to 2 a.m. Pricey, but worth it. (Tel: 516 1616).

We're always willing to make our way to Colonia Reforma, north of the center of Oaxaca, for a meal at the **Casa Oaxaca Café** (Jasmines 518 at the corner of Sabinos, moderately expensive, reservations at 502 6017). Excellent local and international dishes are graciously served in a restful courtyard. Don't miss a sampler of their *memelas,* fresh and hot from the *comal.* Open daily from 8am to 11pm, Sunday from 10 am to 6 pm.

Despite Oaxaca's inland location, you can find **delicious seafood**. The best is at **1254 Marco Polo** (Pino Suárez 806, across from Llano Park, moderately expensive, 513 4308). We love eating in their beautiful garden, shaded by stately avocado trees. The menu includes complex dishes such as filet of huachinango (red snapper) stuffed with shellfish, but we find their simple dishes, delicately seasoned and baked in a wood-fired oven, grilled *a la plancha* or *meunier,* more than satisfying. They stop seating at 6pm, so make a gracious afternoon *comida* your main meal. Marco Polo also serves excellent, reasonably-priced breakfasts. Open from 8am to 6:30pm, closed Tuesday.

Equally good for fish and seafood, but located southeast of the zócalo at Cuahtémoc 206, is **Los Anzuelos** (951 501 1462). Like Marco Polo, they bake their fish in a wood-fired oven. Their shrimp cocktails are first-rate, their filets with your choice of sauce are fresh and savory (heads-up—*al diablo* is *muy picante),* and service is excellent. Tuesday-Sunday noon through 7 pm.

Gourmet treat? You decide. Artist, B&B owner and restaurateur Oscar Carrizosa has opened **Casa Crespo**, a small, very high-end restaurant at Allende # 107, between the Alcalá and Garcia Vigil. He features *"cocina de autor"*--something between imaginative dishes and "ephmeral art," consisting of tasting menus of 5, 7, or 9 courses, starting at $400 pesos. The restaurant has garnered rave reviews, but many locals find that the gourmet tidbits don't match the price. If you're curious, but not game for one of the pricey tasting menus, Oscar suggests that you drop by for a drink and one of the day's menu items. More at www.casacrespo.com.

Chef Jose Luis Diaz was the chef at El Teatro Culinario, the predecessor to Casa Crespo. He's now at the small and very upscale **Hotel Azul,**, Abasolo 313, in the center of town, offering breakfast, *comida*, and *cena*. Dinner can be ordered a la carte, or you can try a 5, 7, or 9 course tasting menu of Diaz's "cocina de autor", starting at $450 pesos. Telephone: (951) 501 0016.

Hosteria de Alcalá (Macedonio Alcalá 307, 951 516-2093, open every day from 8 a.m. to 11 p.m.). You'll find the Hosteria in the beautiful covered courtyard just past the entrance to Amate Books, three blocks north of the zócalo on Oaxaca's main walking street, the Alcalá. While their food is nothing special, it's one of the most romantic places to eat in Oaxaca. The Hosteria is a good place to go late in the evening for one of their flambeed desserts or coffee drinks, dramatically prepared at your table.

La Catrina de Alacalá, at Macedonio Alcalá # 102 email: *lacatrinadeAlcalá@casacatrina.com.mx*, (514 5704). Open Monday through Saturday for breakfast from 8 a.m. to 1 p.m., afternoon *comida* and *cena* from 2 p.m. to 11 p.m. La Catrina is a high-end restaurant featuring Oaxacan specialties that are well prepared and presented. The setting is beautiful--an elegantly redesigned colonial house and two-tiered courtyard covered with a striking dome. Architect and painter Rolando Rojas has decorated the interior with an artist's touch. Although a bit pricey, it's a lovely *ambiente* for a special meal. It's the kind of place where you're likely to see high-level Oaxacan movers and shakers along with their bodyguards. La Catrina de Alcala has recently lost its popular chef. Check locally for the current situation.

Fuego y Sazón is located at 5 de Mayo 306, in Jalatlaco, a cobblestone-paved neighborhood just east of the historic center. If you take a taxi, you can tell the driver that the restaurant is "al lado del Hotel Los Pilares"--next to the hotel Los Pilares. The young owner, Carlos, has created a spacious and attractive dining area, and chef Laura prepares a variety of tasty dishes. We enjoyed her mole negro over chicken, red snapper steamed with savory herbs, and, for dessert, a knock-out dish composed of snippets of homemade flan in a liqueur-based sauce. They pride themselves in making everything they serve from scratch, and it shows. Good food, but definitely pricey, including a $20 peso cover charge. Open from 2 pm to 11 pm Monday through Saturday; bar until 2 am. Reservations at 515 3994; http://www.fuegoysazon.com/.

La Jicara at Porfiro Díaz # 1105 is a delightful small restaurant affiliated with a high-quality bookstore. Their food is imaginative and tasty, and the *ambiente* (atmosphere) casual and a bit bohemian. They feature a good fixed price *comida corrida* Monday through Thursday from 1:30 pm to 4 pm ($70 pesos, $80 on Friday for homemade pasta). Call (951) 516 5638 for dinner reservations.

Comida tipica—Oaxacan specialties

A restaurant that's a little removed from the center but worth the trip is **Los Almendros**, a Oaxacan secret (Tercera Privada de Almendros 109, Colonia Reforma, moderate, 515 2863). The Leyva Carreño family has been serving **typical Oaxacan fare** in a homey environment since 1974. Special dishes change daily, and it's a popular Sunday destination for Sra. Soledad's "*rica barbacoa.*" Open from 1pm to 6pm daily except Thursday.

Las Quince Letras (Abasolo 300, moderate, 514 3769) serves typical Oaxacan dishes in a very pleasant outdoor patio full of grapefruit trees. The food is consistent and reliable, if not exciting, and comida corrida is available daily. Two doors away from the restaurant, on the corner of Av. Juarez, the same kitchen offers **food to go** -a popular alternative for those who wish to dine at home. Open every day from 8am to 9pm except Sunday until 7pm.

We've come to like **El Tipico** in its new location at Zarate 100, between Pino Suarez and Libres (Tele. 518 6557, www.eltipico.com.mx, open 8:30 am To 6 pm daily) It lives up to its name, offering excellent versions of Oaxaca's typical dishes—*botanas* (appetizers), *moles*, *chiles rellenos*, soups, etc., at reasonable prices in a pleasant patio-garden setting.

A restaurant with a theme—actually a philosophy—is **Itanoni: the Flowering of Corn** (Colonia Reforma at Belisario Domínguez 513-Bis, inexpensive, 513 9223). The owner, Amado Ramírez Leyva, believes that corn, domesticated in Mexico 9,000 years ago, is the basis of Mexican culture. He selects particular local varieties, grown in the traditional way, for each dish. You'll see the corn being ground, made into *masa*, pressed into tortillas, and baked on a *comal*. As you sip a delicious corn-based drink and eat the savory *quesadillas, memelas* (like tortillas, only thicker), *tetelas* (memelas stuffed and folded into triangles), *tostadas*, or *tacos*, accompanied by your choice from a dozen or more savory fillings, you may come to agree that you have found "a flavor haven that contrasts with our hurried world." Open Monday through Saturday from 7:00am to 4:00pm, Sundays 8am to 2pm.

Another gem in Colonia Reforma is **Yu Ne Nisa,** offering delicacies from the Isthmus of Tehuantepec. We have to credit Henry, the owner of Amate Books, for alerting us to this hidden treasure. **Yu Ne Nisa** is the creation of Ofelia Toledo Peneda, a native of the Istmus and talented chef. Although Ofelia's menu covers the range from delicate and zesty appetizers, through soups, and on to main courses and desserts, on our first visit we mostly made our way through her appetizers. We had mouth watering *guarnaches*--small tortillas topped with a delicate and delicious filling, flaky *empanadas* with an equally delicate, completely different filling, and two kinds of crumbly cheese eaten on thin, crispy baked tortillas. Ofelia also regaled us with small but very spicy *chiles rellenos*, one of her specialties. We're going to go back to sample more of the menu, but we loved both Ofelia's mole of toasted corn and her yellow mole. Her restaurant, at Amapolas # 1425, in Colonia Reforma, is small, simple, and comfortable. It's posted hours are from 10 am to 6 pm every day, but Ofelia says it's best to call in advance--(951) 515 6982--just to make sure.

If you want something quick and simple, try **Tacos "Alvaro"** (Porfirio Díaz 617 at the corner of Quetzalcoatl, inexpensive, 516 7482). We first ventured in after noticing that it was always full of locals obviously enjoying their food. You can get excellent tacos with your choice of a dozen different fillings (we especially like *al pastor*). But we go back again and again for their superb **pozole**, a rich, spicy hominy-based stew. The *pozole* also makes a great take-away item. Open Monday to Saturday from 3:30 p.m. to 1:30 a.m.; closed on Sunday. A branch is now open at 20 de Noviembre at the corner of Zaragoza from 2:30 pm to 1:30 am.

We're happy to add another *taqueria* to our recommended list–**Los Combinados**---at Reforma 705, near Conzatti Park, and at Emilio Carranza 602 in Colonia Reforma (2:00 p.m. to 10 p.m., closed

Sunday). Their ingredients and condiments such as diced pineapples to add to your taco are fresh and tasty. In addition to tacos filled with your choice of more than a dozen ingredients, Los Combinados also offers appetizing grilled sandwiches and tasty *alambre,* mixtures of sliced meat, veggies, and cheese quickly sauteed into a savory dish.

A local chain offering tacos, pozole, and, in some of their branches, good meat and chicken dishes, is **Don Juanito**.. We prefer the pozole at Tacos Alvaro, but find Don Juanito a convenient alternative. Their new location on Calle Trujano, two blocks west of the zocalo in the home of the former El Naranjo restaurant, has an expanded and more interesting menu.

Of the **cafes on the *zócalo***, our favorite is the **Bar Del Jardin** and its sister restaurant, **La Cafeteria** (west side of the *zócalo*, inexpensive). We can't vouch for their slogan, "The best café in the southeast of Mexico since 1938," but we, along with many locals, find their regional food, drinks and friendly service consistently enjoyable. Try their *tacos dorados* (crispy tacos filled with chicken). Open from early morning until late at night. It's also a great place to hang out and watch the world go by.

A nice surprise is the buffet on Thursdays, Saturdays, and Sundays at **Terranova,**, on the east side of the zocalo. The only drawback is that it's up a long flight of stairs, but the variety and quality of the food is worth the effort. We've been several times and have enjoyed the fresh salads, the many main dishes offered, and the desserts.

Comida corrida—fixed price afternoon meals

Oaxaca has hundreds of small, usually family-run restaurants serving "***comida corrida***," a fixed-price lunch consisting of several courses. The most complete of the *comidas corridas* offer a soup course, rice or pasta, a main dish (often chicken, meat, or some type of enchilada), *agua fresca* (fruit drink), and dessert. We have sampled a number of restaurants (sometimes called *cocinas economicas*)serving *comida corrida*, with a self-imposed limit of no more than 50 pesos per person. You won't find gourmet preparations, and only rarely will you have a choice of what to order, but it's a great deal for the price. Many are closed on the weekends. **Here are the ones we like best:**

Cocina Economica "Isabel," off Pino Suárez at Cosijoeza # 200, offers good value for your peso in a pleasant garden-like setting. Their *comida corrida* features a choce of three starters and five main dishes. They also serve breakfast. Open from 8:30am to 5:00pm Monday through Saturday, closed on Sunday.

Another inexpensive place to eat is **TAYU**, a large restaurant in an attractive space at 20 de Noviembre # 416, across from the market. They offer a *comida corrida* with several dishes to chose from. Our one complaint is the overly-loud live music. Open Monday through Saturday from 8am to 5pm. Tel: 951 516 5363.

El Buen Gourmet, on Av. Independencia 1104 between Av. Juarez and Pino Suárez, is an unpretentious cafeteria-style restaurant featuring many choices. They also have very good (albeit expensive) **roast or BBQ chickens to go.** Open 8am to noon for breakfast every day except Sunday, noon to 5pm every day for *comida corrida*.

At the southeast corner of the *zócalo*, **El Importador's** *comida corrida* offers four courses, with a choice of your main dish, plus *agua fresca* and coffee. We were pleasantly surprised by the quality of the food. Open for breakfast from 7am to noon; *comida corrida* weekdays from 1pm to 4pm; a la carte service until midnight.

El Andariego, in the Hotel Parador San Miguel at Independencia 503, offers two *comida corrida* menus at differing prices in a very pleasant ambiance on weekdays from noon until 5pm. Open from 7:30am to 10pm. You might deviate from the *comida corrida* in order to taste their **crema de hierba santa**, a delicious and unusual soup.

A new restaurant worth trying is **Los Naranjos,**, in the center at Armenta y Lopez #515, open 8am-11pm, phone 951 501 0362. The menu of the day consists of soup, a nice green salad, a choice of two main dishes accompanied by very good rice and beans, fruit water and dessert for 55 pesos. The place is attractive, the service is pleasant, the portions are large, and the food is quite good. They have a wood-burning pizza oven and a fuller menu offering soups, salads, pastas and a variety of main dishes. Those prices are considerably higher than the *comida corrida*.

The place we like best for *comida corrida* is **Casa Elpidia**, several blocks south of the *zócalo* at Miguel Cabrera 413. The contrast between the noisy street and the lush interior garden with its five or six tables could not be greater. Elpidia, who cooks and serves, could not be nicer. And her homemade *antojitos* (appetizers), soups, *arroz*, nicely spiced meat or chicken, and light desserts could not be better. Open every day until 6pm.

We're adding **Cafetería Bander Burger** (Pino Suarez 802, across from the east side of Llano park near Marco Polo) because of their enjoyable and inexpensive *comida corrida*. However, it's also a good choice for breakfast, sandwiches and burgers. Open 8 am to 9 pm Monday through Saturday, 8 to 8 on Sunday.

Donde está el Chef? Everyone's favorite French chef, Jean-Michel Thomas, has launched his new eatery at 407A Eucaliptos in Colonia Reforma. The creperie, **Donde esta mi Crepa?** offers a long list of savory main-course crepes plus a mouth-watering selection of sweet crepes, in a lovely setting. Monday and Tuesday from 2 pm to 8 pm, Wednesday through Friday from 2 to 9, and Saturday from 4 to 9. As always, delicious and reasonably priced.

Non-Oaxacan cuisine

Thai food in Oaxaca! A place where you can find tasty Thai food in Oaxaca is a bit of a secret. It's not a restaurant, but the home and patio of a excellent chef, open to all comers, but only **on the first Sunday of the month** from 1 p.m. to 7 p.m. It's very popular with the resident ex-pats. The house--at Venustiano Carranza # 207 not far from the intersection Cinco Señores--is a bit tricky to find, so call for directions and reservations (recommended) at 503 8134, or (cell) 044 951 216 6790 or 951 509 0626. Look for a sign that says "Casa de Kiji". Call to find out about other Sunday specials.

And real Chinese food too! Expats and long-term visitors here have wished for years for a source of good Chinese food in

Oaxaca. Our wishes have been granted with the opening of **China Beijing** at Jasmines 616 in Colonia Reforma (Tel: 132 5864, open daily from 1 pm to 10 pm, moderately expensive). Owner Zhu Han Wang has imported a chef from Beijing. Wang told us that the chef doesn't yet speak a word of Spanish or English, to which we added that he clearly does speak Chinese food. The menu includes soups plus a substantial selection of what turned out to be mouth-watering rice, noodle, veggie and meat dishes. Enjoy!

Italian food like you would find in Genoa.. Two cousins from Genoa have opened an elegant Italian/mediterranean restaurant two blocks from the zocalo. It's called **Epicuro Cafe Bistrot**, and lives up to its name in terms of epicurian delights, all prepared at the moment. We have gone several times to this new find, have ordered a wide range of their soups, pastas, main courses and desserts, and have always been happy with the service, the food, and the experience. Calle Guerrero #319; www.epicuro.info; 951 514 9750; open every day except Tuesday from 1 p.m. to 11 p.m.

If you have a yen for pizza or other Italian dishes, try **Casa de Maria Lombardo** (Abasolo 304, moderate, 516 1714). Generous salads, well-prepared pastas, and tasty baguettes are also offered. Open from 2pm through 11pm except Sunday until 10pm. Live music is featured on Tuesday, Thursday, Friday and Saturday starting around 8 pm, and Sunday from 3:30 pm to 5:30pm.

Mezzaluna Ristorante at Allende # 113 (Telephone 516 8195, open daily from 2 p.m. to 11 p.m.) joins the above as an enjoyable place for good Italian food, especially their salads and pizzas.

If you're near the *zócalo* and develop a craving for pizza, grab a slice or two to take away at **Don Pizzotte**, in a tiny space at the northeast corner of the square. Owner/chefs Gabriella and Mario Santocchi hail from Umbria. They've lived in Oaxaca for many years, but clearly haven't forgotten how to make a real Italian pizza, hand-made and freshly baked. They usually have four or five classic Italian toppings, plus Hawaiian and spicy *chorizo*. If you're lucky, you may find some of Gabriella's creamy lasagna or Mario's savory foccacia. Open from around 11 a.m. to 9 p.m. most days.

We and our friends consistently enjoy **Comalá** (Allende 109, half a block west of Alcalá, moderate, 044 951 114 2747 and 044 951 168 7062). The menu features a wide variety of reasonably-priced Mexican and American-style food as well as a tasty fixed-price *comida corrida,* attentively served. Open Monday through Saturday from 8:30am to midnight. Good for breakfast, too.

If you want a change from typical Oaxacan fare, try **100% Natural,,** a cheerful restaurant on the south side of Llano Park, dedicated to fresh, healthy food (Dr. Liceaga # 115, moderate, 132 4343). Their juice drinks and smoothies are excellent, as are their hotcakes. They also serve attractively presented salads, sandwiches and wraps, and breakfast is good, too. Open from 7:30 am to 10:30 pm daily.

El Morocco offers an exotic ambience, and zesty Mediterranean/North African specialties at a reasonable price. You'll find their gleaming copper tables and friendly service at Reforma 905-D, just north of Oaxaca's center. Great couscous, lamb dishes and chicken bastilla! Open 8 am to 11 pm daily (www.elmoroccocafe.com; 513 6804.

"Clean, affordable and nice." That's how the friendly owners of **Cafeteria La Principal** describe their tiny new eatery. This is a great place for breakfasts, salads, sandwiches, fresh fruit and juices in a clean, bright space. Pino Suarez # 504, in the center; 132-7765.

Eating Well Outside of Oaxaca

We often end out visits to the *tapete*-weaving village of **Teotitlán del Valle** with *comida* at **Tlamanalli** (Avenida Juárez 39, expensive; 524 4006). Open from 1:15pm to 4pm every day except Monday. (During *Semana Santa,* closed Thursday and Good Friday.)

Abigail Mendoza Ruiz and her sisters make delicious *comida zapoteca* from scratch in their tiled kitchen, open for all to see. You can watch them grinding corn and cooking up your dish. (The sisters give cooking classes at times; inquire when you're there.) Their soup with *chepil*, a tasty traditional herb, makes a great starter. The *mole* with *hierba santa*, a local green with a unique licorice flavor, is excellent, as is their *mole* thickened with toasted

The Mendoza sisters cooking at Tlamanalli

wheat. They make a wicked flan, but their home made ice creams flavored with rose petals or *zapote negro*, a regional fruit, are anven better end to a spicy meal. Our judgment about the quality of the food was vindicated when we spotted Alejandro Ruiz, the executive chef of Casa Oaxaca, bringing four visiting chefs to eat at Tlamanalli!

If you and your friends are really hungry, take a taxi to **La Escondida** (Carretera a San Agustín Yatareni Km 0.7, **just off the highway to El Tule,** moderate, 517 5550 or 517 6655). It's a huge palapa-covered restaurant with hundreds of tables. Local business people go in droves during the week, families and party groups on the weekend. Don't be put off by appearances. Sample its amazing buffet, loaded with fresh salads, excellent soups, a huge range of typical Oaxacan and Mexican dishes, savory grilled meats, and desserts. La Escondida is the best way to sample a wide variety of delicious Oaxacan specialities. Open daily except December 25 and January 1, 1:30pm to 6:00pm.

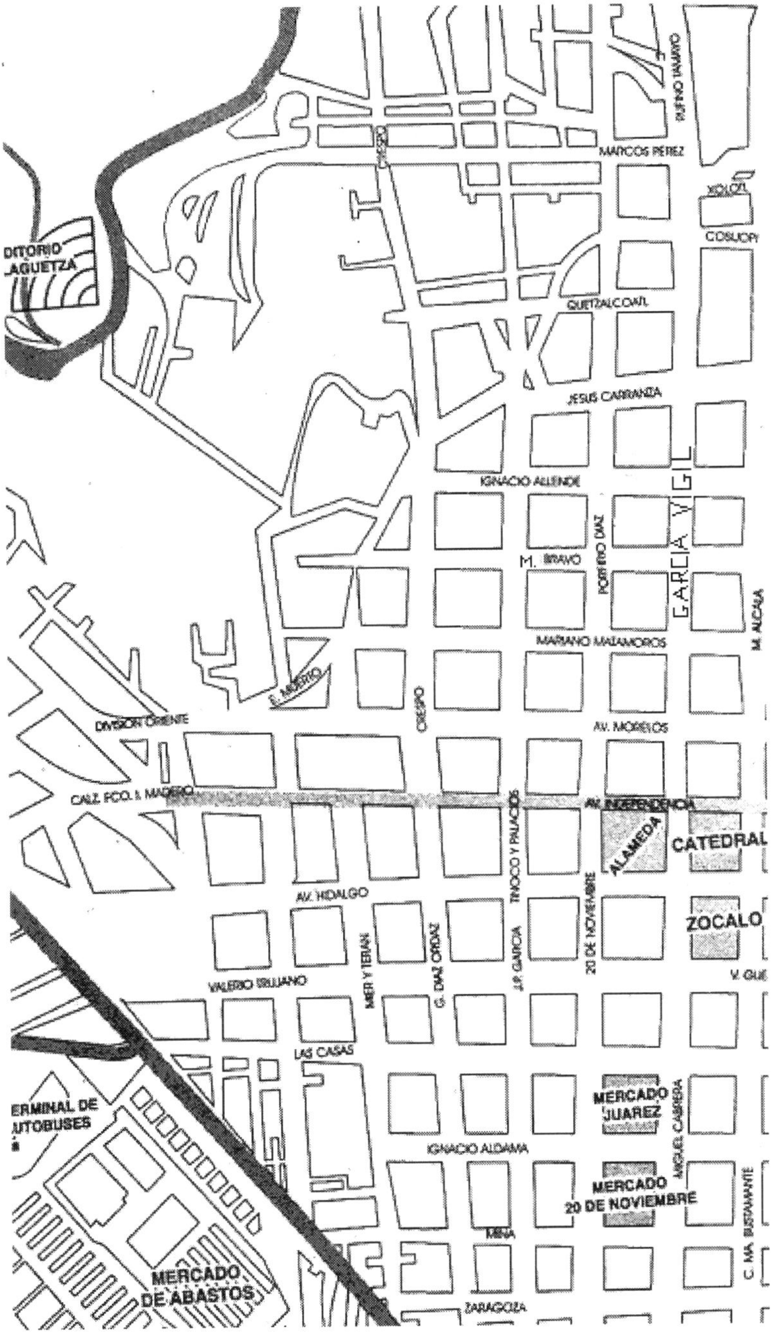
DITORIO
LAGUETZA
RUFINO TAMAYO
MARCOS PEREZ
CRESPO
XOLOTL
QUETZALCOATL
JESUS CARRANZA
IGNACIO ALLENDE
M. BRAVO
PORFIRIO DIAZ
GARCIA VIGIL
MARIANO MATAMOROS
M. ALCALA
DIVISION ORIENTE
AV. MORELOS
CALZ. FCO. I. MADERO
AV. INDEPENDENCIA
TINOCO Y PALACIOS
ALAMEDA
CATEDRAL
AV. HIDALGO
20 DE NOVIEMBRE
ZOCALO
VALERIO TRUJANO
MIER Y TERAN
G. DIAZ ORDAZ
J.P. GARCIA
LAS CASAS
ERMINAL DE
UTOBUSES
MERCADO
JUAREZ
MIGUEL CABRERA
IGNACIO ALDAMA
MERCADO
20 DE NOVIEMBRE
C. MA. BUSTAMANTE
MINA
MERCADO
DE ABASTOS
ZARAGOZA

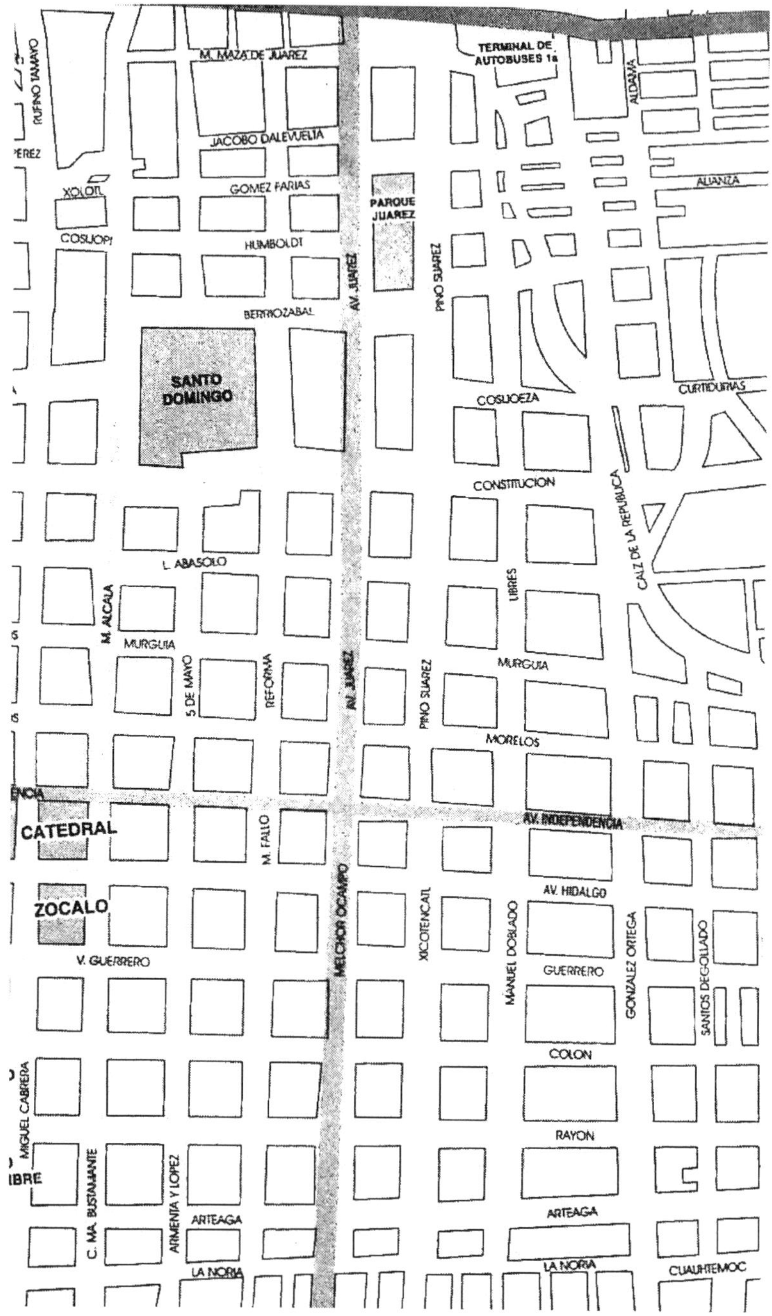
M. MAZA DE JUAREZ
RUFINO TAMAYO
TERMINAL DE AUTOBUSES 1a
ALDAMA
JACOBO DALEVUELTA
XOLOTL
GOMEZ FARIAS
ALIANZA
PARQUE JUAREZ
COSIJOPI
HUMBOLDT
AV. JUAREZ
PINO SUAREZ
BERRIOZABAL
SANTO DOMINGO
COSIJOEZA
CURTIDURIAS
CONSTITUCION
CALZ DE LA REPUBLICA
L. ABASOLO
M. ALCALA
LIBRES
MURGUIA
5 DE MAYO
REFORMA
AV. JUAREZ
PINO SUAREZ
MURGUIA
MORELOS
AV. INDEPENDENCIA
CATEDRAL
M. FALLO
MELCHOR OCAMPO
ZOCALO
AV. HIDALGO
XICOTENCATL
MANUEL DOBLADO
GONZALEZ ORTEGA
SANTOS DEGOLLADO
V. GUERRERO
GUERRERO
COLON
MIGUEL CABRERA
RAYON
C. MA. BUSTAMANTE
ARMENTA Y LOPEZ
ARTEAGA
ARTEAGA
LA NORIA
LA NORIA
CUAUHTEMOC

A bit farther along the same route, at Km 2, lies **La Caballeriza,** an excellent restaurant for meat, including American and Argentine cuts of steak, plus typical Oaxacan dishes. Our Oaxacan friends introduced us to it as a special treat, and we go back at the drop of a fork. It offers relaxed and comfortable dining inside or out on a spacious terrace, and excellent service. (Moderately expensive, 951 517 6477, 1-6 p.m. Daily).

Hacienda/Restaurante Santa Marta (Just off the state road to Nazareno Etla, in San Sebastian de las Flores, about 15 minutes by car or taxi from the center of Oaxaca—look for the old airplane– 521 2835 and 521 2836.) Santa Marta is the sister restaurant to La Escondida. Santa Marta offers lots of outdoor play space for children. Open daily from 1:30 p.m. To 6:30 p.m.

In the small town of El Tule, you can take a break from admiring the famous tree and the charming church to have lunch at **Comedor El Tule** (Andador Turistico Carr. Cristobal Colon number 6, moderate-inexpensive, 518 0089, 9 am to 6 pm). It's an unpretentious restaurant with excellent dishes. We like their *tlayudas, tasajo,* and *chiles rellenos* filled with *picadillo de pollo*. It looks unpretentious, but draws some well-off Oaxacans.

Another great choice **just outside of El Tule** is **La Palapa de Raúl**. Although a little hard to spot, it's on the right side of the main highway heading to Mitla, at kilometer 11 (moderately expensive, 517 5450). They serve the best grilled meats we've had in or around Oaxaca, in an extremely pleasant setting. Bring your friends. Open Monday to Saturday from noon to 7pm, Sunday 8am to 7pm. They now have a **sister restaurant** by the same name in Colonia Reforma at Belisario Dominguez # 251 (8 am to 7 pm Monday through Saturday, closed Sunday, phone 132 6174).

On the **highway from Oaxaca to El Tule**, on the left, at kilometer 11.9, you'll find the unique **Caldo de Piedra—Stone Soup** (moderate). Their signature dish is a fish and/or seafood soup prepared to order in a pre-hispanic manner, by heating river stones in a fire and then dropping them into a bowl containing the assembled ingredients. The soup is fresh and very flavorful. We also savor their *memelas, empanadas* and *quesadillas* made from native corn and hot off the *comal*. Monday through Saturday 8am to 6pm, Sunday noon to 6pm. (cellphone 044 951 550 8486, caldodepiedra@hotmail.com)

In **Zaachila,** we've enjoyed *comida* at **La Capilla,** a large, shaded outdoor restaurant, popular with bus tours, featuring a wide selection of regional food (moderately expensive). This may be your chance to sample *chapulines* (spicy fried grasshoppers), a Oaxacan specialty. However, we have been warned that eating chapulines puts one at risk for lead poisoning, so be advised!

Before or after the colorful Sunday market in **Tlacolula,** we enjoy breakast or *comida* at **El Sazon de la Abuela** (23 Francisco Madero, inexpensive, 562 1902). The restaurant is in a spacious, attractive courtyard, and lives up to its claim of providing excellent regional cuisine including scrumptious *pan dulce* (typical pastries).

If you're going to be in **Etla,** for example for their market or to visit **CASA,** the beautiful ex-paper factory that's now an arts center, you can find excellent regional dishes at **Chefi,** in the Villa de Etla at Avenida Morelos 44. We thought that their black mole was one of the best we've had, as were their chiles rellenos. Chefi serves authentic Oaxacan food.

Another good option near **Etla** is **Mia Arroz,** which we think offers the best Chinese food in the region. This unassuming indoor/outdoor eatery is on the right side of the *Carretera Internacional,* the main highway from Oaxaca to Mexico City, just before the turnoff to San Sebastian Etla. Open Tuesday through Sunday, 2 p.m. through 7 p.m. Call first to be sure they're open: 521 3395, www.mexonline.com/miaarroz.htm

Coffee, chocolate, and pastries

Searching out the best places to drink coffee or buy beans is a favorite pastime for many visitors. Here are a few places that offer consistently good coffee and hot chocolate, Oaxacan style. Many also offer pastries or light lunch food.

Nuevo Mundo, at M. Bravo 206 (501 2122), is an excellent bet. They roast and brew delicious coffee (including decaf), usually have a good supply of tasty house-baked items on hand, and offer a pleasant space to hang out (and use your laptop). If you're going to brew your own coffee at home, try one of their blends. We like their *mezcla de la casa,* or house blend. They also make good hot chocolate, but be sure to specify that you want *"chocolate oaxaqueño."* Open from 8am to 10pm Monday through Saturday, until 2pm on Sunday.

Café Gecko (inside the courtyard at 5 de Mayo 412, 516 2285) offers good hot chocolate and coffee in a quiet covered patio on Monday to Thursday from 10am to 9pm, Friday and Saturday from 10am to 2am, closed on Sunday.

A welcome addition to the Oaxaca coffee scene is **La Brujula** ("The Compass," Garcia Vigil 409-D, cellphone 044 951 526 0056). Hosts Kyle and Berenice have created a cozy spot for breakfast, sandwiches, and other light fare. Kyle, using some great family recipes, turns out savory waffles, sinfully good cinnamon rolls, and even bagels. They also sell their excellent coffee in bean form. Open 8am to 9:30pm Monday through Friday, weekends 9am to 4pm.

Another welcome addition to the Oaxaca café scene is **Gozobi** (Garcia Vigil 504, 516 2938). Walk past the bar in the entrance to the tranquil shaded patio, complete with trickling fountain. Gozobi's menu features salads, baguettes, pastas, and crepes, a wide variety of tea and coffee drinks (including flavorful decaf), plus a full bar and roof terrace. Open 8am to 11:30pm, closed Tuesdays.

Hotel Casa Vertiz (Reforma 404, 516 1700), roasts and serves high-quality coffee from Chiapas. You can also get excellent pastries made in house, and served at graciously spaced tables in the hotel's restaurant, **Las Nubes.** Open from 8am to 10pm Monday through Saturday, 8am to noon on Sunday.

Many visitors and locals enjoy **Café La Antigua** (Reforma 401, 516 5761). They take coffee seriously, serving all organic and Pluma coffee, and also provide a comfortable *ambiente* for coffee, snacks, and a chat. Open Monday through Thursday 9am to 10pm, Friday and Saturday 9am to 11pm, closed on Sunday.

You'll find outlets of the mega-chain **The Italian Coffee Company** in many locations around town, including (among others) across from Santo Domingo church, on the northeast corner and the west side of the *zócalo,* and on the south side of Llano Park. It's hard to argue with their coffee, but we were not happy to find that they make hot chocolate—one of Oaxaca's specialties—with an Italian syrup. You can order any of their hot coffee drinks with decaf, but don't expect great flavor. Service tends to range from casual to indifferent, especially at their *zócalo* shop.

We also ran into the chocolate syrup problem at the gleaming **Café del Teatro** adjacent to the **Teatro Macedonio Alcalá** (5 de Mayo near the corner of Independencia, 514 3548). It's a lovely place to go before or after a theater event, but stick with the excellent coffee and other treats. Open 8am to 11pm daily.

If you're near Conzatti Park, spend some pleasant time sipping coffee in the colorful, art nouveau-ish **Arabia Café** (Reforma 117, corner of Jacobo Dalevuelta, 515 9886). Good breakfasts, excellent baguettes, including a dynamite smoked salmon and cream cheese combo, good salads, and a variety of tisanes are offered. Open from 8:30am to 11:30pm daily, 4pm to 11pm on Sunday. One of our favorites!

And northeast a few blocks, at Curtiduria 117-A in Colonia Jalatlaco, stop at brand new **Bor Bon.** The feature a wide variety of teas, excellent coffee and coffee drinks and good snacks.

Oaxaca is gradually modernizing, as you'll see in the newly renovated **Plaza San Jeronimo** at Alcalá # 316, just across from Amate books. There you'll find **Black Coffee & Gallery,** plus a branch of **Cinnabon** –go figure--and a pricey store for women's accessories.

At some restaurants or cafes you may see **café de la olla** or **café Oaxaqueño**. This is usually brewed by heating coffee grounds, cinnamon, and sugar in an urn. When well made, it's delicious.

You can find good, standard ***pan dulce****—Mexican style pastries*--at Pan Bamby on García Vigil, or at any one of a number of bakeries on Independencia. **Pan & Co.** in Colonia Reforma at Belisario

Domínguez 612, in the first block west of Heroico Colegio Militar, makes a variety of mouth-watering **European breads and pastries**, using only natural ingredients, plus a variety of **fruit teas**.. Luckily for denizens of Oaxaca's center, there's **a branch at Allende 113-A,** at the corner of Garcia Vigil, which also serves coffee you can drink while you munch your cinnamon roll. The hours at the Allende shop are from 9am to 9pm, while the main store opens at 8am. Both branches are closed on Sunday.

Farther north in Colonia Reforma, at Amapolas 1519, you'll find the well-named **La Pasión.** Its owners, Corrado Schlaepfer and Florence Prevot, fashion European pastries, cakes and quiches that would grace a shop in Paris, which you can take away or enjoy on site along with coffee or your choice from a wide variety of gourmet teas. Open Tuesday to Sunday 10 am to 10 pm; 513 8100. Since it's a trip, call to make sure they're open.

Safe and Savory Street Food!

It took us a while to muster up the courage to try eating the way thousands of *Oaxaqueños* do—munching a crisp *tlayuda* or a savory *memela* hot off the *comal* at one of Oaxaca's many street stands. Like most visitors, we were worried about getting sick. However, street food stands often produce extremely fresh, tasty Oaxacan specialties that would be a shame to miss.

Oaxacan friends have taught us how to select **street stands** that produce food that is safe to eat. Look for places that draw large numbers of people day after day, are staffed by more than one person, and where the person handling the money is not also doing the cooking. (Or, if it is the same person, be sure that he or she always uses a plastic glove when handling money.)

Friends invited us to have **breakfast** with them at the stand run by **Doña Inez, on J.P García** three blocks south of the *zócalo*, along the west side of the Artisan's market. We loved it and go back as often as we can. Inez prepares delicious, crispy folded *tlayudas* with a mouth-watering *salsa* inside, and equally savory *memelas*, slightly thicker folded tortillas stuffed with your choice of ingredients. You can take your selection with you, or eat it right then and there, sitting on plastic stools set out along the sidewalk.

Another very popular street stand nestles alongside of **Templo San Agustin**, on Guerrero near the corner of Fiallo. It's been a fixture for 15 years, and consistently draws crowds to snack on its highly recommended *memelas, tlayudas* and *empanadas*. We like their filling of *chorizo con papas* — spicy sausage cooked with potatoes -- and their *carne con salsa verde* -- meat with green chile sauce.

Alongside stately **Carmen Alto** church, just across García Vigil from the **Casa de Benito Juarez,** you'll find another long-established and popular street stand offering a similar range of savory goodies to eat there or take away.

Few tourists seem to make it to **Jardín Conzatti**, which is a shame since it is a very pleasant park. If you are one of the few, though, you will usually find a colorful trailer at the southeast corner of the park. Known as **La Hormiga** – the Ant -- it is famous for its tasty tortas (sandwiches). You can spot it by the line of hungry locals.

For a somewhat surreal nighttime eating experience, wander over to **Calle Libres between Murguia and Morelos**. A large stand magically appears there at around 9:30pm. Line up with the hungry *Oaxaqueño*s, order *tlayudas* with your choice of ingredients, sit down at one of the tables in the patio, wait for your order to be brought to you, and enjoy.

Another nighttime-only stand appears at the corner of Bustamente and Arteaga after 6:30 or so most evenings. Tasty *tlayudas* and bounteous *blandas* are prepared to order on the *comal*. If you're lucky, you'll get a seat. If not, sit on the curb or in doorways along with everyone else.

If you're on the street at night, you'll probably pass local women selling *tamales* with various fillings out of deep metal steamer pots. These are almost always delicious and safe to eat. Two of our favorite vendors are along the north side of Abasolo, a few blocks east of Alcalá. Another well-known *tamalera* can be found on 20 de Noviembre at the corner of Hidalgo. The *tamale* vendors start to show up around 8pm, just in time for *cena*.

Entertainment

We always enjoy just hanging out at the *zócalo*, with its sidewalk cafes, wandering musicians, strolling families, and constant buzz of activity. We love the **free concerts by the State Band of Oaxaca** (Sundays at 12:30pm and several nights of the week at 7:00pm) and the **State Marimba Band** (Mondays and Saturdays at 7:00pm, Wednesday at noon and *danzon* at 6:30pm, and Friday at 12:30pm). Evening at the *zócalo* brings a constant stream of *trovadores* (singers) and *maríachis*.

The following **nightspots** feature live music (but note, these venues change their offerings frequently). Telephone numbers for many of these places are hard to find, but we've listed them where we can.

Café Café, Tinoco y Palacios 604, Thursday through Sunday in a romantic outdoor setting around a fountain; **Café Central**, Hidalgo 302, alternative cinema Wednesday, jazz Thursday, other live music Friday and Saturday, starting at 9pm; **Candela**, Murguia 413, 514 2010, great for *salsa* and dancing Thursday through Saturday from 10pm to 2am; **Cielito Lindo**, Morelos 511, offering *trova* (guitar ballads) Tuesday through Thursday and larger groups Friday and Saturday; jazz at **Hipotesis** next door; **Free Bar** at Matamoros 100-C; **La Cucaracha**, Porfirio Díaz 301-A, *trova* Monday through Saturday and Latino disco music and dancing Thursday through Saturday; **La Parroquia**, M. Bravo at Porfirio Díaz, 516 6469, live music Fridays and Saturdays from 10pm to 2am; **La Salamandra**, Cinco de Mayo 110; **La Tentacion**, Matamoros 101, 514 9521 from 10pm until the wee hours Tuesday through Sunday, with salsa Thursday through Saturday; and **La Nueva Babel**, Porfirio Díaz 224, every night starting at 9:30pm, featuring jazz, *trova*, blues, funk, and classical guitar. A new place for drinks, snacks, and music is **La Cantinita**, at Alcalá 303. You can recognize it by the enormous serpent stretched across the wall of the front room. La Cantinita is a fresh and lively addition to Oaxaca's night life (open from noon to 4am every day, 516 8961). Be sure to check out the bathrooms!

Although Oaxaca is the state capital and a major cultural center, information about upcoming events is in short supply. It pays to keep an eye out for **posters advertising special events** and also to check the helpful **calendar at www.oaxacacalendar.com/**. We've seen great folkloric dance performances for free; knock-out concerts by world-famous virtuosi; and concerts by Oaxacan native and Oscar-nominee **Lila Downs,** and another soulful *Oaxaqueña,* **Susana Harp.** Oaxaca has a truly elegant space for drama, dance and music in the beautifully refurbished **Teatro Macedonio Alcalá..** Catch an event there if you can.

If you're not in town for the **Guelaguetza** in July, you can get a taste of regional music, dances and costumes in shows presented at the **Camino Real Hotel** (Cinco de Mayo 300) on Fridays at 7:00 pm, or nightly at 8:30 pm at the **Casa de Cantera** (Dr. F. Ortiz Armengol #104, in Colonia Reforma, (951) 515 3768, www.casadecantera.com). Prices range from $150 to $360 pesos per person, depending on where you go and if you choose to eat there. Check times, dining options, and prices in advance.

Pineapple dancers from Tuxtepec

If you're looking for relaxation and rejuvenation, try a **temazcal,** a pre-Columbian combination of sauna, aromatherapy and massage. A friend of ours scheduled one at **La Casa de María**

(Belisario Domínguez 205, Colonia Reforma, 515 1202) and returned several hours later glowing, relaxed and refreshed.

Another long-established temazcal is **Manos Indígenas de Oaxaca** (Reforma 402, email bugambilias@lasbugambilias.com or call 516 1165 to reserve). A very authentic version of a *temazcal* can be arranged through *curandera* (healer) **SeZora Nieves** (Juárez 58, Teotitlán del Valle, call 524 4151 to schedule). Please note that since the heat treatment takes place in a dark, womblike space, it's definitely not for claustrophobes.

If a *temazcal* doesn't appeal to you, you can have your choice of a wide variety of massage techniques at **Namaste**, Constitución 100-3. You can drop in, or call in advance at 516 9645. Prices are in the $600 range. The latest in stress relief seems to involve *piedras calientes* (hot stones) or a whole-body chocolate rub.

Friends who have been treated by holistic masage therapist **Gisela Camarillo Duran** swear by her. She apparently has both the training and the touch to help with aches and pains, and also with more serious or long-standing bodily problems. By appointment only: 518 0217 or 506 0489; cel: 951 190 3934. Her office is at Periferico # 306, in the Chedraui shopping center, Local 3-C. Price around $350.

Another widely-recommended place for massage is **Casa del Angel**, at the corner of Jacobo Dalevuelta and Calle Reforma, on the northeast corner of Conzatti Park. Prices are in the $300 range. Yoga classes are also available here.

Shopping

Oaxaca and its surroundings are a **paradise for shoppers**, especially those who appreciate handicrafts. The shops contain examples of many kinds of work, reflecting the ethnic and artistic diversity of the state. Wonderful things can be found at the various markets, in stores, and from individual vendors near the *zócalo* and on the streets around the markets.

You can find **barro negro** (black pottery) from **Coyotepec**, *barro verde* (green-glazed pottery) from **Atzompa**, *barro rojo* (red pottery) from **Tlapazola, cotton weavings** done on waist looms from **Santo Tomás Jalieza,** wool *tapetes* woven on wooden looms from **Teotitlán del Valle,** *alebrijes* from **Arrazola** and **San Martín Tilcajete,** carving from **La Union,** etched **pottery** from **Ocotlán,** and **intricately embroidered blouses and dresses** from throughout the state.

The prices in the markets are almost always significantly lower than in the stores, and the vendors in and around the *zócalo* offer prices which are often lower still. In the stores the prices are fixed (maybe you can negotiate a small discount), but in the markets and on the streets it is expected that you will bargain.

The opening price is usually fairly reasonable, considering the amount of time and effort that have gone into making the item. Generally you can settle on a price about 70% of the initial offer. Please don't undervalue the work of the artisan by offering an insultingly low price or by saying that you don't like something that is being offered to you. As long as you admire the work and offer a price that reflects your appreciation of its value, you can engage in the art of bargaining without offending anyone.

Most stores open by 10am, close for lunch around 2pm, re-open around 4pm, and stay open until 7pm. Note—times are flexible!

Good places to start are the largest galleries, to get an idea of what is available and what "standard" prices are like. These stores all sell a wide variety of well-made handicrafts: **La Casa de las Artesanías,** at Matamoros 105 on the corner of García Vigil (9 am to 8 pm Monday through Saturday, 10 am to 6 pm Sunday); the newly-opened **La Plaza,** next door on Matamoros; **MARO,** a cooperative of women artisans located at Cinco de Mayo 204 (9:30 am to 8:30 pm Monday through Saturday, 9:30 am to 7:30 pm Sunday); and the recently re-located **Instituto Oaxaqueño de las Artesanías** (formerly known as ARIPO), south of the zocalo at Dr. Pardo #2 (9 am to 7 pm Monday through Friday, 11 am to 3 pm on Saturday, closed on Sunday). These galleries consist of several rooms around a central courtyard, each of which features a different handicraft. The colonial architecture of the buildings alone is worth a visit.

La Mano Mágica, on Alcalá, stocks a smaller variety of regional crafts. It is also possible to find *tapetes* from Teotitlan here.

At García Vigil 512, in the building occupied by La Biznaga restaurant, you will find several high-end shops. Our favorite of these is **Chimalli**, which features Day of the Dead figures, *alebrijes*, and tin work at reasonable prices. You will also find amazingly intricate ceramics by the well-known **Castillo family**. You can expect to pay top peso at these stores, but you'll go home with top quality items. Packing and shipping available.

El Nagual, at 5 de Mayo 402-A, near Santo Domingo church, features a carefully selected assortment of fine folk art, handwoven clothing and *tapetes*, and contemporary graphics. The *tapetes* by Erasto "Tito" Mendoza Ruiz are exquisite. This is a must stop for shoppers with a taste for the best. You can get a sense of their offerings at http://elnahualfolkart.blogspot.com.

At 5 de Mayo 408-7, a small shop called **Amara** has a lovely selection of whimsical jewelry, featuring the designs of Gabriela Sanchez.

Just down 5 de Mayo, at the corner of Abasolo, you'll find **Guapinol**, featuring ***ambar*** (amber) jewelry. Unlike the amber that you may be offered on the street, this is the real thing.

Oaxaca is known for its delicate ***filigrana*** (filigree) jewelry, and **La Marquesita**, at Valdivieso 120 (just behind the cathedral), has an extensive selection of this art form. You can find elaborate pieces with pearls, coral, and colored stones.

Across the street from the Camino Real Hotel are several shops selling tin work, silver, *alebrijes*, weavings and paintings. The collection of *alebrijes* at **Hecmafer Bazar Artesanal,** Cinco de Mayo 301, is of the highest quality we have seen in Oaxaca. They also have a large selection of ceramics by the Castillo family.

Around the corner from Santo Domingo, on the south side of the **Plazuela de Carmen Alto**, you can find an occasional treasure at **Artesanías Cosijo,** in the back rooms of the blue house. Owner Teodoro López Jimémez stocks an array of carvings, masks, ceramics, and whimsical tin pieces, some of very high quality. Teodoro will pack and ship large or delicate items for you.

Two stores offering high quality goods at prices to match are **Tempero,** at Cinco de Mayo 101, and **Sierra Morena**, at the back of the Plaza de las Virgines, bordering Labastida Park on Calle Abasolo. Tempero has a good selection of large, heavy, colorful cotton *rebozos* as well as the lovely Tehuana blouses, and also features contemporary styles combined with traditional weavings and embroidery. Sierra Morena offers a large selection of woven and embroidered bags, *huipiles*, blouses from the Tehuantepec region, and the largest supply of *rebozos*, of all colors and materials, that we have seen.

Also in the Plaza de las Virgenes you will find a store called **Terra Quemad**a (Burned Earth). The ceramics are made by various members of the same family, and are a synthesis of traditional materials and modern designs. Each piece is a knock-out.

If you're interested in cool, **linen clothing**, take a look at the shops at Alcalá 503 and also in the **Santo Domingo Plaza** (corner of Alcalá and Allende). The Plaza is also home to a store featuring silver jewelry from Taxco, and the very lovely shop of **Jacobo and Maria Angeles**, a master carver of *alebrijes* from San Martin Tilcajete. Their shop, **Corazon Zapoteco**, also has elegant examples of **handicrafts from other regions of Mexico.**

Guatemalan crafts are represented in two stores in Oaxaca, **Etnico Textiles** at Allende 113 and its sister shop at Gurrion 104, both within a stone's throw of Santo Domingo church. Here you will find examples of Guatemalan weaving in bedcovers, pillow covers, huipiles, bags, etc.

Nearby, at Gurrion 110, you'll find high-style versions of *ropa tipica* at the shop of **Silvia Suarez.**.

For elegant clothing and shoes, the **Oaxaca Raizes** store in the Plaza los Geranios at Garcia Vigil #304 should not be missed. **Tehuantepec–inspired** silk rebozos, purses, and clothing are on offer, along with the very popular **San Miguel shoes.**

Another source for these popular and very comfortable shoes is from the **Senora de los Zapatos, Loty Mendoza (English-speaking)**. Shoes are on display at the Hotel Las Mariposas, Pino Suarez #517, and Señora Mendoza can also bring a selection of styles and colors in your size to you at your home or hotel. Call her at 517 5263 or (cell) 044 951 126 5549 to set up a visit.

One of our favorite shops for *ropa tipica* is **La Calenda**, at Tinoco y Palacios 303, slightly off the main tourist trail. Their prices tend to be a bit lower than at many of the other shops. You'll find a wide selection of beautifully embroidered blouses, skirts, *huipiles*, and bags. The owner, Abby, is particularly helpful.

Along the shady side of Alcalá you will find the five García López sisters, and sometimes their mamá as well, selling lovely **hand-embroidered blouses and dresses**. You can find similar items in shops and the markets, but you can easily pay twice as much for them there versus negotiating with the *hermanas* García López.

A recent addition to the Oaxaca shopping scene is **Federico**, at the corner of Tinoco y Palacios and Matamoros, in the *esquina azul* (blue corner). Looking more like a store you might find in Santa Fe, New Mexico, Federico offers a beguiling combination of southwestern turquoise jewelry, English silver, antique shawls and *huipiles*, and silver-trimmed saddles. Most of their clients are well-off *Oaxaqueños* who are intrigued by these carefully-selected items from "abroad."

When in El Tule to see the famous tree, eat at the Comedor El Tule (see **Where to Eat** section) and then walk down the street away from the plaza to a store called **Ayuuk** (Carr. Cristobal Colon #1, 518 1000). Ayuuk carries **handicrafts from the Sierra Mixe**, including the distinctively embroidered blouses and shirts from the town of Santa Maria Tlahuitoltepec. You can also find a selection of interesting ceramics from the Mixe region.

You should also spend some time in the markets just south of the *zócalo*, looking at food as well as handicrafts. **The 20 de Noviembre market** sells bread, cheese, chocolate, mole, and other regional delicacies and has *fondas* (casual counter restaurants) featuring home cooking. The **Benito Juárez market** has innumerable stalls selling food, flowers, leather goods, knives, clothing, baskets, and other types of handicrafts, as does the enormous **Abastos market**, south of the center of town. Don't miss the **Mercado de las Artesanías**, southwest of the *zócalo* at the corner of J.P. García and Zaragoza. This indoor market has handicrafts from all over the region. You'll also see women dressed in traditional *huipiles*, weaving on waist looms.

On your way to the Mercado de las Artesanías, you will pass an unremarkable doorway at J.P. Garcia #601. If you look just inside the entry, you'll see the usual display of black pottery, and won't think there's much of a reason to go inside. But, there is! **Bengali** is a treasure trove of **wearable weavings from Mexico and Guatemala**, where you will find wonderful huipiles and beautiful blouses in an enticing environment.

Chiles at the Abastos market

You'll see even more women in exquisite *huipiles* at the **Mixteca market** that takes place in the narrow street bordering Labastida Park, between Alcalá and 5 de Mayo, every day from mid-morning to late at night. Trique-speaking vendors offer hand-embroidered blouses, dresses, woven bags, and much more. You can find many of the same goods at the **Mercado de las Artesanías and in shops,** but the market is fascinating.

One of our favorite ways to shop is just to wander the streets and markets near the *zócalo* chatting with the vendors, and comparing prices at the various *puestos* (stands). You will be approached by vendors who walk around the *zócalo* offering their hand-made jewelry, weavings, *rebozos* (shawls), embroidered blouses, carved wooden combs, fans, paddles, spoons, hot chocolate beaters, bookmarks, cocktail toothpicks, hotpads, etc.

The prices offered by these vendors, especially for the woven items and jewelry, are very reasonable compared to the prices in the shops and markets. If you see something that interests you, it's well worth taking a look and doing a little bargaining. Plus, you get the opportunity to speak with the artist!

A word of warning: the *"ambar"* for sale on the street is rarely the real thing. Don't let the trick with the lighter fool you! Real amber is light weight, and feels warmish to the touch. False amber is heavier than the real thing, and quite cool to the touch.

Oaxaca is also a mecca for artists and art lovers. In addition to the galleries discussed below, you can read about more **art outlets, openings and current expositions** in the monthly **Guiarte** guide, available for the asking at most galleries. If your Spanish is adequate, you'll find lots of information about the arts scene in the monthly **El Jolgorio**, also free around town.

There are many distinctive galleries featuring contemporary art scattered around the historic center. In addition, you will generally find an outdoor artists and artisans' market in **Labastida Park**, as well as a number of interesting small galleries in the Plaza las Virgenes, bordering the park at Labastida 115.

For **contemporary art**, the following galleries stand out: **Galeria Indigo**, Allende 104; **Galeria Quetzalli**, Constitución 104-1; **Galeria 910**, on the second floor of Alcalá 305; **Sonrya Galeria**, Alcalá 102; **Arte Biulu**, Aldama 100 in Jalatlaco—well worth the visit; and the wonderful **Arte de Oaxaca** at Murguia 105.

In addition to handicrafts, don't forget to take home some of the fabulous **chocolate and *mole*** for which Oaxaca is famous. **Oaxacan chocolate** contains cacao, sugar, cinnamon and almonds. The proportions of each ingredient vary, forming the basis for your choice. The chocolate is fairly granular and is mainly for use in cooking or making hot chocolate, rather than intended for just eating – but of course there's no law against that! **Moles** are available in red and black, generally in a paste-like consistency. You prepare them at home by adding chicken broth and/or tomato sauce and/or Oaxacan chocolate.

In and around the **Benito Juárez market** you will find stores and stands selling these products. The major brands are **Mayordomo, Soledad, and Guelagüetza**, although many lesser-known brands are available as well. The "big three" have stores on 20 de Noviembre and on Mina, where they will offer you samples so you can select whatever tastes best to you. Everyone seems to have a favorite brand of chocolate and *mole*. Some of our Oaxacan friends prefer the chocolate from **"El Jarrito"** at the Pasillo de Contingencias #14, inside **Abastos Market,** to any other brand. Our favorite brand of chocolate is **Calenda,** which we find melts better and is less granular than the others. One local woman we know—a great cook—believes that Mayordomo makes the best chocolate and Soledad makes the best *mole*. We prefer Guelagüetza's *mole*, so there you go.

Convenient convenience store: Mayordomo chocolates has installed a reasonably well stocked convenience store in front of their restaurant at Alcalá # 302. We can't recommend the restaurant, unless you are traveling with young children who will enjoy playing in the restaurant's playroom, at the back of the large dining hall. You can get coffee, hot chocolate, and pastries in the pleasant coffee shop, also in front of the restaurant.

Getting to Oaxaca

Although we see U.S. and Canadian license plates, most North Americans get to Oaxaca by air through Mexico City. Airlines serving Oaxaca from Mexico City include **Aeromexico, Aviacsa and Mexicana** (assuming bankrupt Mexicana restructures and resumes operations in 2011 as advertised). A better alternative, if it works from your departure point, is **Continental Airlines'** currently daily non-stop flights between Houston and Oaxaca. (**Note:** many Mexicana passengers have arrived in Oaxaca without their luggage due to problems with baggage handling in Mexico City. You might consider another carrier if you have to go through Mexico City, or fly Houston to Oaxaca.)

Smaller airlines that fly between Oaxaca and other Mexican destinations include **Aerotoucan** (www.aerotucan.com.mx/), **Azteca** (www.abstravel.com/airlines/azteca.shtml), **Avolar** (www.despegar.com.mx/airlines/avolar.html) (+52 954.582 0151) and **Volaris**..

Relatively low-cost Volaris (www.volaris.com.mx) uses Toluca as its hub, and flies from there to most of the important cities in Mexico. The round trips linking Oaxaca and Tijuana--just across the border from San Diego, and with connections to Los Angeles, Oakland and San Francisco--can be surprisingly inexpensive.

Vivaaerobus, another low-cost airline, offers flights to Oaxaca from Monterrey and Mexico City. It's currently advertising flights as low as $350 pesos (around $30 U.S.)! From the U.S. call 1-888-935 9848, or visit their website at:
http://www.vivaaerobus.com/mx/todoslosdestinos.htm

Once you arrive at the Oaxaca airport, the best way of getting into town is via the airport shuttle service, **Transportes Terrestre**. As you head out the door to leave the terminal building, stop at the booth, tell them where you're going, and buy a ticket. You will be directed to the appropriate van, based on your destination. A one-way ticket to your hotel or other address in the center costs $48 pesos per person within the historic center, $88 if farther out. Make sure you have pesos to pay with.

Note: Normal taxis are not allowed to pick up passengers at the airport. A few intrepid travelers hike out to the main highway and flag down a cab there. We don't recommend this, since you'll actually end up paying more.

To get back to the airport from the city center, the easiest and cheapest way is to sign up a day or two ahead for a van that will pick you up wherever you are staying. Drop by **Transportes Terrestre** a bit south of the main post office, at Alameda de León 1-G across from the Cathedral (514 1071, open 9am to 2pm and

5pm to 8pm, **closed Sundays**). The cost going out to the airport is the same as the cost coming in: $48 pesos per person from the historic center, $88 pesos from farther out. If you take a taxi to the airport instead, it may be more convenient, but will cost about $130 pesos from the city center.

Getting around—transportation and guides

Helpful **maps of local bus routes** are available at Amate Books and at the Oaxaca Lending Library. Current bus fares are $5.50 pesos. It's helpful to have change.

If you're only going to be in Oaxaca briefly, you can easily find your own way around town thanks to the helpful maps of the *centro historico* (historic center) handed out by hotels, shops, the **main tourist office** next to the Secretariat of Tourism at Murguia 206, between Cinco de Mayo and Reforma, and the tourist kiosks near Santo Domingo and the Cathedral. You can go anywhere in the historic center on foot.

For slightly longer trips, for example to **Colonia Reforma** or to the movies and shopping at **Plaza del Valle**, or **Plaza Oaxaca**, you can easily flag a taxi or take a city bus. Oaxacan taxis don't have meters, so you'll need to **agree on a price before getting into the taxi.** Announce where you want to go and ask, *"Cuanto cuesta?"* You shouldn't need to pay more than $30 or $35 pesos within the center, or more than $45 or $50 to an address on the outskirts.

If you need to call for a taxi or arrange for one in advance, we recommend **Sitio Alameda** at (951) 516 2685 or (951) 516 2190; or **Sitio ADO** at (951) 515 1503 or (951) 516 1572, or **TAXI EXPRESS** at 518 7479. These are good numbers to keep at hand.

Guided tours are probably the best way to see the surrounding sights for the first time. We have had good luck with the **Agencia de Viajes Marques del Valle**, in the **Marques del Valle Hotel**, on the north side of the *zócalo*, and with **Continental–Istmo Tours,** at Alcalá 201 (516 9625), but there are many other tour companies offering similar partial and full day trips, as well as private guides who will customize a trip for you. You may be able to sign up at your hotel. Most tour companies will pick you up where you are staying and take you around in van-sized groups or, for a higher fee, provide a dedicated car and guide.

We haven't tried them yet, but **Another Oaxaca: Tours that go beyond**, offers tours that promise to go a bit deeper into what the region has to offer in terms of traditions and culture, and also in how contemporary Oaxacans live and work. You can read a description of their philosophy and scheduled tours at: http://www.traditionsmexico.com/beyond/index.htm.
Email: traditionsmexico@yahoo.com; (951) 514 4131.

Another good source of help with travel arrangements and tours in or around Oaxaca is **Viajes Paradiso**, headed by charming, energetic, and multilingual (French-English-Spanish) Marie-Noëlle Monsch. Viajes Paradiso is located in the Plaza de las Virgenes, at Plazuela Labastida 115, Interior 9A. Telephone/fax: (951) 516 6967 or 516 3061. URL: .http://viajesparadiso.com/
Email: viajesparadiso@yahoo.com.mx.

For a **general guide** to Oaxaca, you won't find anyone better than **Pablo Gonzalez** (cellphone 044 951 134 7391, email: marsch@prodigy.net.mx). He is both a **bird expert** and a top-notch guide to Oaxaca, its surroundings, and the rest of the state. He's fluently bilingual, a safe driver, very knowledgeable, relaxed, and, as a bonus, very funny. We call on him frequently.

Friends who have used the services of **Luis Ramirez**, a driver who is studying to become a licensed guide, recommend him highly. His English is good and he knows the region well. You can reach his cellphone at 044 951 118 4534; email: taxi136@hotmail.com.

If you don't feel the need for a guided tour or English-speaking driver, you can hire a taxi to take you anywhere in the region and wait for you, for about $150 pesos (roughly $12.50 U.S.) per hour.

Autobuses Turisticos, across from the **Hotel Rivera del Angel,** at Mina 501, provides direct transportation to and from **Monte Albán** once an hour from 8:30am to 3:30pm for $40 pesos. Last return from Monte Alban at 5 p.m. (951) 516 5327.

If you're a bit more adventurous, you can get to nearby *pueblos* by taking a bus from the **second-class bus station** just off the Periferico, west of the **Abastos Market.**. Although the bus station is huge, its entrance is just a gap between two vendors' stands. Once you're at Abastos, ask for directions to the "*Central Camionera,*" and once inside, ask for the *puesto* selling tickets to your destination. You can get to Zaachila, Teotitlán del Valle, and other craft and market towns this way. If you're planning to go to Ocotlán, it's better to take a bus from **Transportes de Ocotlán**, on Miguel Cabrera near the corner of Zaragoza. Buses leave Oaxaca every 8 to 10 minutes.

Another option for heading out of town is to take a "***colectivo***," a taxi that collects a load of passengers and takes them all to a particular location. *Colectivos* heading south and east park on an extension of Victoria Mercaderes south of Abastos market. Those heading north and west congregate along the extension of Valerio Trujano north of Abastos.

Detailed **maps** are available for sale at **Amate** Books. *Colectivos* heading east to Teotitlán and Tlacolula stop on the Calzada de Niños Heroes, at the corner just east of the baseball stadium (*Estadio de Beisbol*). Each *colectivo* displays the name of its destination on the front windshield. You can also catch *colectivos* back to Oaxaca from outlying towns, but check the time of the last return trip.

Colectivos typically pack two passengers into the front seat along with the driver, and four in back. If you don't want to be that crowded, it's perfectly acceptable to tell the driver that you want to pay for two seats for each member of your party. Or, you can hire a *colectivo* as an *exclusivo*, meaning it will carry only your party. Ask the driver for the price.

Another option is to hire a taxi by the hour or day. You can hail a taxi and negotiate the price, or call one of the **sitios** (taxi stands) in advance. We've had consistently good service from **Sitio Alameda** (951) 516 2190, and **SITIO ADO** (951) 516 0503.

More distant destinations, such as **Puerto Escondido, Puerto Angel, Huatulco, Puebla, or Veracruz**, can be reached by vans, first-class buses, or, in some cases, by airplane. The **first-class ADO bus terminal** is at Calzada Niños Heroes de Chapultepec #1036. You can also reserve seats and buy tickets at **Ticketbus**, at 20 de Noviembre #103 and other locations around town.

Information and tickets for flights **to the coast** can be obtained from travel agencies, or directly from the **Aerotucan office** at Alcalá 201 (502 0840), or **Aerovega** (516 4982) at Alameda de Leon #1, near the post office . The cost of a half-hour flight to **Puerto Escondido** is more than $200 per person round trip, but it can be a good alternative to the notoriously curvy bus ride over the mountains. Alternatively, pop a Dramamine, take the bus and, ideally, sleep the whole way to the coast.

It is also possible to take a van to the beaches, via a shorter but curvier route than the buses take. Information on the vans can be found at **Atlantida**, La Noria 101, near the corner of Armenta y López, or at **Servicio Express** at Arista 116 (516 4059). Atlantida vans go to Pochutla. From there you can take a taxi to the beach towns. Servicio Express goes all the way to Puerto Escondido. Consider taking a dose of Dramamine before leaving.

Rental cars are readily available, but tend to be a bit pricey. We've found good service, well-maintained vehicles and reasonable prices at **Alamo**, 5 de Mayo #203-a in the historic center. Local numbers: 514 8534 or 515 8686. You can also try **Hertz** at the airport or in town, telephone 516 2434, or **Europecar**, at Matamoros 101, (52) (952) 516 9305.

Learn some Spanish, or Oaxacan cooking, or cha-cha-cha

Oaxaca is a great place to study Spanish. It has a dozen or more language schools, plus many private tutors. Oaxacans are amazingly patient responding to even the most basic Spanish. Even a week or two of classes can kick-start your Spanish skills and give you a great entree into the Spanish speaking world.

The **Instituto Cultural Oaxaca (ICO)** at Juárez 909 has a particularly beautiful campus, on the grounds of a former hacienda. The institute's fees include afternoon *talleres* —workshops-- in weaving, pottery,salsa dancing and cooking. (515 3404 or 515 1323; www.inscuioax.com). Expect a full schedule!

The similarly named **Instituto de Communicación Internacional (ICI),** at Murguia 805 opposite the Merced Market, also has a good reputation. Unlike the ICO, it does not offer extras such as dancing or cooking classes. You can contact the director, Omar Nuñez, at 503 8257.

A long-time *Oaxaqueña* friend strongly recommends **Academia Vinigulaza** at Abasolo 503 (www.vinigulaza.com; 513 2763).

Oaxaca Spanish Magic, at Berriozábal 200, is headed by a dedicated and highly motivated teacher, **Flor I. Bautista Carreño.** (516 7316; cellphone 044 951 557 0962; www.oaxacaspanishmagic.com). A large number of visitors and expats attend and recommend Flor's teachers and her school.

Most schools offer a choice of small classes or private instruction; a mixture of grammar and conversation; the opportunity to stay with a local family; and *intercambio*, person-to-person chats with locals who want to practice their English. Tours, plus dance and cooking classes, can also be arranged, generally for an additional fee. Classes usually start on Mondays. Some schools will let you sign up for as little as one week at a time, while others require longer commitments.

After checking out several schools, I (Robert) picked **Becari** at M. Bravo 210 (www.becari.com.mx, 951 514 6076) for my first lessons because of the flexibility and friendliness of the staff as well as its convenient location and moderate cost (from $150 per week). Along with a dozen or so other new students, I took a brief written test early on Monday. We were soon sorted into classes appropriate to our Spanish skills, with three or four students per teacher. Becari suggests two hours of grammar and two hours of conversation per day, but offers more or less intensive programs.

It was fun, and it worked. Within two weeks I was using past and future tenses, reflexives, and other niceties that previously had not graced my middle-school Spanish.

Potential students seeking a rich cultural exchange should check out **Ollin Tlahtoalli** at Melchor Ocampo 710. They provide Spanish instruction, content classes on Mexican history and literature, plus a variety of volunteer opportunities, for example helping Oaxacan children and artisans to learn English. More at www.ollinoaxaca.org.mx; (951) 514 5562.

We've heard rave reviews from several students at **Español Interactivo** (Armenta y Lopez 311-B, 514 6062, telephone from the U.S. 213 634 1444, www.studyspanishinoaxaca.com). The school provides an intensive, highly structured and very interactive program that can really jet-propel students' progress. They also offer many cultural experiences, excellent, hands-on cooking classes, and accommodations in friendly local homes.

For individual lessons, I (Robert) warmly recommend **Spanish tutor Laura Andrea Olachea Magriña.** Telephone: (+52 951) 514 7094; cell: 044 951 128 8411; Email: spanishclassesoaxaca@gmail.com; website: www.spanishclassesoaxaca.sitioprodigy.com.mx.

Those of us who study with Laura feel lucky to have her here in Oaxaca. She's an intelligent, well educated and well traveled woman whose teaching style is energetic, engaging and enjoyable. She's great at adjusting what and how she teaches to each student's needs. She's also very flexible in terms of the timing, length and frequency of lessons, and all at a very reasonable hourly price. Laura has also pioneered the use of **video Skype calls** to allow out-of-town students to continue their lessons with her.

Laura likes to work one-on-one with individual students, or with couples. **Note:** she's very popular, so contact her well in advance!

Another well-recommended private tutor is **Claudia Ángeles Valencia.** Claudia can be reached locally at 516 0724, via her cell at 044 951 169 1264, or at: angelesclaudia@hotmail.com.

An enjoyable way to improve your Spanish and get to know locals is to drop in at the **Oaxaca Lending Library**'s free weekly **intercambio**, every Saturday at 10 a.m. You'll be paired with a local who wants to improve his or her English. Pino Suarez # 519.

Cooking classes

Many language schools offer optional cooking classes; check with your school for particulars. We loved our **Becari–sponsored cooking class** and I (Jo Ann) learned to make great black *mole*.

We consistently hear rave reviews about the cooking classes offered by internationally famous chef **Pilar Cabrera** (516 5704; Email: infor@casadelossabores.com; direct from the U.S. (201) 255 6104; http://casadelossabores.com).

Author, chef and television personality **Susana Trilling** provides highly acclaimed one day, long weekend, and weeklong cooking classes at her center in Etla, Rancho Aurora. Contact her well in advance at **Seasons of My Heart** (From the U.S. 011 521 951 508 0469; cel: 044 951 508 0469; local (951) 508 0044 or 504 8100; info@seasonsofmyheart.com). Susana also organizes regional culinary tours; details at www.seasonsofmyheart.com. A friend of ours, a chef in his own right, interned with Trilling for several months and speaks highly of her skills.

We've heard very positive reviews about the half-day cooking classes offered by the chef and owner of elegant **Casa Crespo** (Calle Crespo # 415) and the restaurant by the same name at Allende # 107. Reservations at +52 (951) 516 0918 from outside Mexico, or (951) 514 1102 from within Mexico, or by email at: casacrespo@go-oaxaca.com. Classes demonstrating traditional Oaxacan dishes cost $65 U.S. per person, and those featuring contemporary delicacies typical of the restaurant cost $110 per person. For $25 per person, participants can invite guests to join them to dine on the delicacies the class has produced. One long-time resident told us it was the best meal she'd had in Oaxaca. An Website: http://www.casacrespo.com/cookingclasses.html.

More interested in eating than cooking? B&B owner Alvin Starkman offers expertly guided culinary tours of the region. Details at http://www.oaxacaculinarytours.com/ ; Telephone from Canada or the U.S. 011 52 951 132 8203; email: info@oaxacaculinarytours.com.

We haven't tried them, but the full-day classes on **prehispanic cooking** offered by chef **Agustin** in English, Spanish or French sound interesting. Contact him at: agustin@tasteofoaxaca.com.

Salsa, Merengue, Cumbia and Cha-cha-cha

Want to learn to shake it with the best? Sign up for dance classes with Carlos Vargas, a prize-winning instructor, at the **Academia de Baile**, at Lic. Verdad # 108, between Pino Suarez and Calzada de la Republica; Telephone 132 5059; cellphone 044 951 118 3121; www.elsalondelasalsa.com.

Another highly-thought of dance instructor is **David, a former folkdancing professional.** He offers small group classes at his home in the nearby town of Huayapam, combining yoga, breathing exercises, and meditation and aromatherapy with his dance instruction. His 90 minute classes, combining a spiritual approach with shaking your booty, are offered at 70 pesos per session. Call him at 540 8060 (English spoken). Many people love his classes.

More casual drop-in salsa clases can be found at **Candela**, a night spot at Murguia 413 in the center. Clases start around 9 pm on Thursdays, Fridays and Saturdays and cost $50 pesos.

Exercise:

If you're a Pilates aficionado and are here long enough to want to keep up with your workouts, we can recommend Magpilates Estudio at Blvd. de la Paz #101-C, in San Felipe del Agua, a taxi ride north of the center. They have a variety of packages to chose from. The facility is well staffed, well run, and spotless. http://magpilatesoaxaca.com/(951) 520 25 02.

Aurobics Fitness Gym at Constitución 300 (Tel: 514 2608) gets positive reviews from visitors who work out there. You can join for as short a time as two weeks ($450 pesos) or a month ($600 pesos). They offer high quality machines, weights and classes.

Centrally located at Allende 211 between Porfirio Díaz and Garcia Vigil, **Calipso Fitness Center** (Tel. 516 8000) also provides a clean environment, plenty of machines and weights, but no groups or classes. You can by a package of 10 visits for $434 pesos.

Eco-tourism

If you're interested in more **nature-oriented activities,** you cancontact **SierraNorte** (M. Bravo 210; 514 8271; email to sierranorte@oaxaca.com; www.sierranorte.org.mx.) SierraNorte represents the **mountain village of Benito Juárez** and the other *Pueblos Mancomunados*—in the Sierra Norte that jointly maintain hiking and mountain-biking trails and provide simple accommodations and food. We've greatly enjoyed their hikes, usually guided by a personable young (Spanish-speaking) *campesino*. They provide great views and an introduction to this unique group of self-governing, environmentally minded *pueblos.*

You can get to the *Pueblos Mancomunados* on your own by bus. At the second-class terminal, near Abastos, at the last booth on your left, you can buy tickets for one of the blue and white *Flecha del Zempoaltepetl* buses, which leave at 8am and noon.

View from a hiking trail in the Sierra Norte

Tierraventura at Abasolo 217 also offers hikes and tours. Claudia Schurr and Yves Chavan organize ecotours of from one to four days to the outlying, highly indigenous regions of Oaxaca, including the *Pueblos Mancomunados,* or farther afield to Chiapas and the Yucatan. One of their specialties is traditional medicine. Details on their web site is www.tierraventura.com; +52 951 501 1363. They ask that you reserve a week in advance.

Continental-Istmo Tours at Alcalá 201 (516 9625) also offers ecology and history oriented tours to the Sierra Norte. Details on the website at www.continentalistmotours.com.

Experienced, English-speaking **Carlos Rivera Benetz**, founder of **Turismo Aventura,** guides similar treks throughout the state, including a four-day hike to an isolated coffee *finca*. He will also help you with the logistics for self-guided tours, and hook you up with experienced (and fearless) **mountain bike guides**. Email: ecofito@hotmail.com; cellphone: 044 951 180 8143; www.rnet.com.mx.comercios/benetz/index2.php.

You can also **rent mountain bikes** at **Zona Bici** (Garcia Vigil #406, telephone 516 0953, 10 a.m. to 8:30 p.m. (closed Sunday). Or, you can arrange for trail rides or trekking on **horseback** through **Horsebackmexico.** Contact Mary Jane or Roberto. From the U.S. 310 929 7099; in Oaxaca (951) 516 7860; cel 044 951 199 7026; email horsebackmexico@mac.com; www.horsebackmexico.com.

*B*iologist **Fredy Carrizal** at ecologiaoaxaca@yahoo.com.mx (515 3305, cellphone 044 951 103 3175) and **Roque Antonio Santiago** at roque_antonio740@hotmail.com (524 4371) offer individualized tours. Friends who came to visit us spent two days **birding** with Roque Antonio near Teotitlán del Valle and the mountain community of Benito Juarez. They returned home tired but thrilled, with lots of birds to add to their life lists.

Oaxaca is a great place for birding. One expert recently spotted 300 species in the state of Oaxaca state in eight days.

Mezcal—Oaxaca's answer to tequila

We hadn't been in town a day before hearing Oaxaca's unofficial philosophy: *"Para todo mal, mezcal. Para todo bien, tambien."* For everything bad, mezcal. For everything good, the same. Like tequila, **mezcal** is made from fermented maguey plants, but it has a distinctive smoky flavor. Much of it is still hand-made in tiny, family-run distilleries. Tequila, on the other hand, is produced in factories using a process that purists claim is inferior to the slower, more organic approach used in making *mezcal*. Oaxacans are currently trying to create a niche for high quality *mezcal* similar to the gourmet market for single malt scotch.

Maguey has been domesticated in Mexico for thousands of years. While the indigenous people of Mexico learned how to ferment maguey into *pulque*, it was the Spanish *conquistadores* who provided the technology to distill the native *mezcalli* into high-octane *mezcal*. At 76 proof and up, it can pack quite a punch.

Making *mezcal* properly takes a great deal of time and effort. The heart of the maguey is cooked for several days in a stone-lined pit, fueled by a wood fire. After cooling for a week or so, it is fermented in wooden containers for up to two weeks. The resulting liquid is then distilled, traditionally in clay pots.

Mezcal comes in many varieties, including *minero* (double or triple distilled); *blanco*, clear and the least smoky-tasting; *gusano* (with a maguey worm in the bottle); *pechuga* (infused with various fruits and a chicken breast); *reposado* ("rested," or barrel-aged two to six months); *añejo* (aged six months to a year); and *reserva* (aged, usually in American or French oak barrels, for up to several years, and typically very smooth).

Yet another type of mezcal is *tobalá*, which is made from a type of maguey that grows wild at high altitudes. We've been told that a lot of what's sold as *tobalá* is not the real thing. We think it tastes and smells a lot like turpentine, but you may love it.

After getting many contradictory recommendations, we decided to follow the advice of a friendly Oaxacan musician who clearly has a taste for *mezcal*. "Just ask for the "*mezcal de la casa*, (the house mezcal)," he said, "it's usually the best."

One way to drink *mezcal*, we learned, is to rub a few drops of lime juice on the back of your hand, sprinkle the wet spot with *sal de gusanito* (don't ask!), then take a lick before each sip. Or, you can shake a little of the *gusanito* salt right onto the lime, take a nip, and then drink some mezcal.

The many flavors of mezcal

There are any number of places around town where you will be invited to taste *mezcal*, especially around the market and along the *Andador Turistico*. Good places to learn about *mezcal* and try some free samples are the **Plaza de Mezcal** at Matamoros 103 and the **Casa de Mezcal** at Flores Magon 209. You can sample *tobalá* at **Tobalá Mezcal de Oaxaca**, on Murguia, Letter F, at the corner of 5 de Mayo. For a very non-commercial introduction to *mezcal*, drop in at the **Union de Palenqueros de Oaxaca** at Abasolo 510. You'll probably meet Francisco Monterrosa Morales, who comes from a long line of *palenqueros* -- *mezcal* makers.

In stark ontrast to traditional artisanal *mezcal* production, the international corporation Coca Cola-CIMSA has opened an industrial scale *mezcal* factory, CASA AGP, on the road to Tlacolula. They're scaling up their production from 15,000 liters to 45,000 liters daily, and marketing it under the Zignum label. You'll see their ad when you arrive at Oaxaca's airport.

What you'll need in Oaxaca

During our stays in Oaxaca we've eaten at a wide range of restaurants, street stands, and market stalls without getting sick. However, if you're worried, you may want to bring a stash of your favorite digestive aids. We typically bring a supply of **Cipro** just in case we happen to run into a particularly nasty bug. If you start on any antibiotic, it's important to continue taking it for the full course of treatment. Immodium, Pepto-Bismol, and Alka-Seltzer are popular over the counter remedies available at every *farmacia* (drug store).

Note: to avoid over-use of Cipro or other antibiotics you may bring with you, which can lead to the development of drug-resistent bacteria, they should be used only if you are sure you are not allergic to them, are seriously ill, and have good reason to think the source is bacterial (e.g. you associate the onset of your illness with something you ate or drank). Once you start on an antibiotic, you should take the full course specified by a doctor or pharmacist.

Mexican law has recently changed, and it is no longer possible to buy antibiotics over the counter; a doctor's prescription is required. **Farmacias de Ahorro,** which has many branches around the city, has come up with a painless way of accomplishing this: they have installed doctors in *consultorios* adjacent to most of their branches. The doctor will take your history, ask about your symptoms, and even examine you...for free! You will be given a presciption for the medications the doctor thinks you should take, which is then passed to the *farmacia* next door, and the helpful clerk will bring you the medications and ring up your purchase.

Unfortunately, central Oaxaca is a very noisy place. Between barking dogs, screeching brakes, clanging church bells, and frequent fireworks, getting a good night's sleep can be difficult. Even if you're a sound sleeper, you might want earplugs.

During the winter, in town, you probably won't be bothered much by mosquitoes. But if you come during the rainy season, stay in a lushly planted place, or travel to the coast, you'll want a mosquito repellent with an adequate dose of deet.

Oaxaca is just seventeen degrees north of the equator. Even in midwinter, it's easy to get too much sun. So bring a hat and high-powered sunscreen. At 5,100 feet above sea level, the temperature can range from cool in the morning and at night to hot in mid-afternoon. We find it handy to wear layers of clothes to take off or put on as neeeded. Many women wear *rebozos*, locally-woven shawls, which look great and are easy to adjust.

The best way to see the city of Oaxaca is on foot. But Oaxaca's cobblestones, uneven curbs, and desperately-in-need- of-repair sidewalks are tough on shoes and feet. Bring walking shoes or sandals that you know are sturdy and comfortable. Visitors and residents alike quickly learn to keep your eyes on where you're walking to avoid a twisted ankle or a tumble.

Water

First of all, **don't drink the water.** Don't brush your teeth with it, don't rinse your mouth with it, and don't clean your toothbrush with it. Keep your mouth closed when you're taking a shower. Use only bottled water for your teeth, for drinking, and for making coffee or tea. If you somehow inadvertently swallow a bit of tap water, don't panic: a tiny bit won't kill you.

This advice is not a product of prejudice or paranoia. Unlike in the USA and Canada, water in Oaxaca is not pumped continuously through constantly pressurized mains. The *municipio* sends water through antiquated, leaky mains to homes and businesses once every few days. When there is no water in the pipes, contaminated ground water seeps back into them. The water that comes into our house is often brown from dissoved material and sediment.

Besides being unsafe to drink, Oaxaca's water is in scarce supply. Oaxaca suffers from a constant water shortage. Many residents and businesses have to purchase additional water, at great expense, from private companies that truck it in and deliver it through giant tubes *("la pipa")*. You may see these trucks, painted with *"Agua para uso humano,"* delivering water in front of homes and businesses. This water is of no better quality than the water provided by the city; it's just more expensive.

Do your hotel, landlord, and the earth a favor by using only what you really need. You can help by taking shorter showers (with your mouth closed, of course), flushing only when necessary, and being frugal with the water you use for hand laundry.

It's also important to **disinfect any raw fruits or vegetables you buy** before consuming them. On our landlady's very good advice, we soak all of our fruits and veggies for at least 10 minutes in a solution of water and **Microdyn**, a disinfectant available in most grocery stores, following the directions on the bottle.

Medical matters

For a **medical emergency** or to get an **ambulance**, call **065**, or the Mexican Red Cross, **Cruz Roja**, at 516 4455 or 516 4003.

We haven't needed to use a hospital or clinic, but we've been assured by many Oaxacans and long-term residents that you can get good in- or outpatient treatment at any of the following, **all of which offer services 24 hours a day, 7 days a week:**

Clinica Médica 2002, at Emiliano Zapata 316 in Colonia Reforma, **telephone: 515 7200, 513 1169, or 513 7440.**

Hospital Molina, in the center of town at García Vigil 317, **telephone: 516 3836 (outpatient) or 516 5468 (hospital).**

Hospital Reforma, also in the center, at Reforma 613, **telephone: 516 0989, 516 6090, 516 6100, or 514 6272.**

Clínica Hospital Carmen, in the center, at Abasolo 215, **telephone: 516 2612, 516 0027, 516 4468, or 514 2889.** (Staffed largely by the Tenorio family, **English spoken.**)

You will be expected to pay in full at the time you are seen at the clinic or by the doctor. If you have insurance that you think may cover your expenses, request a statement from the doctor showing your diagnosis and treatment, along with a copy of your bill marked "paid," and submit these documents to your insurance company on your return home.

Pharmacy: Las Farmacias de Ahorro keep late hours and will deliver: 515 0000. **Farmacias Omega** also provide good service. They have outlets in the center at Las Casas 111-D, and in Colonia Reforma on Porfirio Diaz across from the Fountain of the Seven Regions They'll also deliver to your address; call 516 6641.

The following **medical specialists** come well recommended:

Cardiologist: Emilio Ambrosio, at Colon 410, Suite 9, 516 1352 or 514 0257; pager: 512 9020, key 6008.

Dermatologist: Rosa María Chavez, at Hospital HMCH at Eucaliptos # 401, corner of Amapolis, in Colonia Reforma, 518 5418.

Ear, nose, throat & allergy:: If your need to see an ENT or allergy specialist, **and your Spanish is adequate**, we highly recommend **Dr. Alberto Garnica Castillo**, at Calle Valdivieso #116, Interior 10, very close to the zócalo. His telephone is 514 6990, but he sees people in the order of their arrival at his office. His hours are 4 p.m. to 8 p.m. Monday through Friday, 10 a.m. through 2 p.m. on Saturday. Dr. Garnica understands English, but feels that he does not speak it well enough to treat patients who speak English only.

Gastroenterologists::

Jose Armando Jiménez Ricardez, 516 0026 (**English speaking**)..
Raul Marin Pineda, Garcia Vigil # 317, 516-6454

Luciano Tenorio, Clinica el Carmen, Abasolo #213 (Interior #2), 501 0477 (after 5:00 p.m.)

Raul Luis Valle, Crespo # 803, 501-0438.

General Medicine:

We noticed that several our friends looked a lot slimmer than the last time we saw them. Their secret? **Dr. Alberto Zamacona Esparza**, a congenial, perfectly bilingual internist and Diplomate in Obesity and Nutrition. Everyone who goes to him recommends him highly. Office at Libres 604-B, in Oaxaca's center. Tel: 513 6422; Cell: (044) 951 130 8730; *dralzamacona@yahoo.com*. Dr. Z. even makes house calls!

Marco Antonio Calleja, Belisario Domínguez 115 in Colonia Reforma, 515 3492 **(English speaking)**). Like many doctors in Oaxaca, he sees patients on a first-come, first-served basis. Office hours are 9:30 am to 2:30 pm, then 5:30 pm to 8:30 pm.

Javier Guzman, Sabinos 204 in Colonia Reforma, 515 3516 **(English speaking)**.

Gynecologists:

Cesar Wong and Adriana Ortiz, at José López Alavez in Colonia La Cascada, 515 2060.

Tzatzil Ayala Barahona, at Clinica Santo Domingo, Alcalá 808, 513 2600 and 513 0060 **(English speaking)**.

Ophthalmologist: Aleta Hayton, at Calle de los Libres 310, 516 4690 **(English and French speaking)**.

Dentists:

Martha Canseco Bennetts, at Tinoco y Palacios 307-2 (**by appointment only, English speaking**, cell: 044 951 198 9473).

Daniel Tenorio Oda, Abasolo 213, 516 0834 (**English speaking**).

Luis Pombo Rosas, Reforma 203-A, 516 6575 or 514 6712. Highly recommended dentist/dental surgeon. "Painless," "High-tech cleaning equipment." By appointment only.

Juan de Dios Porras, at Belisario Domínguez 115 in Colonia Reforma, 513 3614.

Kuri and Sanchez Farid Mena, father and son, at Eucaliptos 204 in Colonia Reforma, 514 1828 and 516 3669 respectively.
Luis H. Martínez Noriega, at Matamoros 600, 516 2765.

Faisal Abdala, at Callejón del Carmen 101, at the corner of Crespo, cell phone 044 951 184 9385 **(English speaking)**.

Martha Ortega Garcia, at Escuela Naval Militar 402-A, Colonia Reforma, 513 0413 (**English speaking**))

Rafael Medina, at Cielo #203, Colonia Lomas del Creston, 513 9520. Highly recommended for modern dentistry, including implants.

Veterinarians:

Luciano Balthazar Carrasco, Carretera Internacional #804, Colonia Pueblo Nuevo, cellphone 044 951 112 1131. His office is a bit far, located on the road to Mexico City at the second pedestrian bridge past Brenamiel, but people who use him swear by him.

Guillermo Perez Ramirez, Calzada Porfirio Díaz # 241-C, Colonia Reforma, 515 2159, or for emergencies, 515 6894. Dr. Perez is a UNAM-trained vet, and, according to his patients, "a great guy."

The dozen best things to do in Oaxaca

1. Hang out at the *zócalo* and watch the world go by.

2. Visit **Santo Domingo Church** and its great **museum**.

3. Take a guided tour of the **Ethnobotanic Gardens**.

4. Take a guided tour of mysterious **Monte Albán**.

5. Catch a **Sunday noon concert of the State Band of Oaxaca**; watch couples performing **danzón to the music of the State Marimba band** on Wednesdays at 6:30, both at the *zócalo*.

6. Check out the **Alhambra–like courtyards of the Hotel Camino Real**, plus the 400-year-old ex-convent's **beautiful fountain-laundry area** in the northeast corner of the complex.

7. Have a **drink at dusk on the veranda of the Hotel Victoria** overlooking the city and its surrounding hills.

8. Visit **Teotitlán del Valle** to see wool being spun, dyed and woven into intricate tapetes. **Eat at Tlamanalli.**

9. Visit the **ruins at Mitla** with their unique "Greca" stonework.

10. Go to one or more of the **nearby villages for *tianguis*,** or outdoor market day: **Etla** on Wednesday, **Zaachila** or **Ejutla** on Thursday, **Ocotlán** on Friday, **Tlacolula** on Sunday.

11. Dive into **Oaxaca's colorful covered markets: Benito Juárez, 20th of November, and Abastos.** The outdoors Friday market held in Llano Park, and the organic market in the churchyard in Xochimilco, the neighborhood just north of the center of town, on Fridays and Saturdays from 8 a.m. To 4 p.m , are also fun.

12. Visit and try to catch an event at the beautifully restored **Teatro Macedonio Alcalá.**

Facts, Figures and Handy Things to Know

Location: Three hundred miles southeast of Mexico City and 120 miles from the Pacific Coast, at 5100 feet above sea level.

Population: 265,000 in the city proper, 515,500 in the greater metropolitan area, and 3,507,000 in the state. The state is home to 16 distinct ethnic groups comprising roughly 40 percent of the total population. Zapotecs, Mixtecs and Mazatecs, in that order, account for 70 percent of the indigenous population.

Money: You'll need to buy pesos. There are plenty of *cajeros automaticos* (ATMs) in the banks on Garcia Vigil just north of the *zócalo*, plus *casas de cambio* near the *zócalo*. The exchange rate has recently ranged from 11 to 14 pesos per U.S. Dollar. You can check current rates at www.xe.com/ucc/.

Books and bookstores:

Libros Amate, or **Amate Books,** in a beautiful colonial building at Alcalá 307, is the primary source of English-language books and magazines in town, including a great selection of books about Oaxacan crafts. It more than accomplishes its mission of offering the best possible selection of titles in English about Oaxaca, Mexico and Latin America. Highly recommended.

La Proveedora Escolar, at Independencia 1001, has a large inventory of books in Spanish.

If you're going to be in Oaxaca for a while, we recommend joining the **Oaxaca Lending Library,** a block below **Llano Park** at Pino Suárez 519 (www.oaxlibrary.com, 518 7077). They offer one, two and three month or yearly memberships. The collection contains 30,000 books, audiotapes and videos in English. There is a pleasant patio where you can find notices about **apartments for rent,** services, and what's happening in Oaxaca, and chat over coffee and bagels with other English speakers, including many knowledgeable long-time residents. It's a great source of information and contacts. You don't have to be a member to use their wireless internet service, although a donation is requested, or to attend their excellent educational programs. The Library also sponsors free *intercambio* -- chats between English and Spanish-speaking visitors – on Saturday mornings at 10. Open 10am to 2pm and 4pm to 7pm Monday-Friday, 10am to 1pm Saturday, closed Sunday and Mexican holidays.

Safety: The horror stories that you may have read about violence in Mexico almost all stem from a few border cities such as Ciudad Juarez. We still consider Oaxaca to be a safe and secure place to visit, explore and enjoy. However, as with most destinations around the world, commonsense precautions are advisable.

The general emergency number is 066. In the unlikely event that you need to speak to the municipal **police**, call (951) 514 4525, 516 0455, or 516 0400. **State police:** (01951) 551 0199.
In case of **fire**, call (951) 506 0248 or (951) 549 2197.

You can find the U.S. State Department's latest **travel alert** at http://travel.state.gov/travel/cis_pa_tw/pa/pa_4491.html.

In the historic center during the day and usually well into the night, there are plenty of people around, as well as a substantial police presence. However, outside of the usual tourist areas, and at times when fewer people are around, unpleasant incidents can occur. At least one person we know of was robbed of her cellphone and camera while walking alone in the late afternoon on Cerro del Fortin, the hill above the city of Oaxaca.

Several people we know, including experienced long-term residents, have been robbed through a **scam** that involves one person surreptitiously smearing or squirting their clothes with an unpleasant substance, for example mustard, and another, perhaps a block away, "noticing" the problem and offering to help by cleaning up the mess. If this happens to you, don't let anyone "help" by patting your clothes clean. Just say **NO!** in a loud, clear voice, repeat that if needed, and walk away. This is one situation where you do not need to be polite!

In short, please be alert—for example after withdrawing money from an ATM-- and try to avoid isolated spots or times where you might be at risk.

Political activity: Oaxaca is one of the poorest and most indigenous states in Mexico. In addition it was the center of a dramatic political upheaval in 2006. Many people who want to help are drawn here. Helping through volunteering, donations, and other non-political involvements can be useful and gratifying.

However, anyone wanting to come to Oaxaca to become involved politically needs to be aware that **the Mexican constitution expressly forbids foreigners from interfering in Mexican political matters.** Anyone doing so can be summarily deported. This doesn't happen often, but it does happen.

Much more seriously, as the murders of independent photojournalist Brad Will in 2006 and of activist Marcella Grace in 2008 tragically show, Mexican politics can be fatal. So come to Oaxaca to experience and enjoy the rich mix of cultures, or to help in non-political ways, but not to become involved politically.

Mail: The main post office is located on Alameda plaza at the corner of Independencia, just north of the *zócalo*.

Packing and Shipping: It's expensive, but if you need to ship goods back home, try PAKMAIL, at Garcia Vigil 504, Local 1 (516 8196; www.pakmail.com.mx).

Shopping hours: Almost all stores and offices close between 2pm and 4 or even 4:30pm, then reopen for business into the evening. Many stores are closed on Sundays.

Buying music: You can buy CDs of Oaxacan, Latino, and World music in dozens of locations around town. The place we've found where the staff will take the time to help you listen to and select what you want is **el sonido Discotheque,** just off the *zócalo* at Avenida Hidalgo 608. The owner, Guisela Katz de Karminsky, is particularly knowledgeable and helpful.

Street Vendors: We very much enjoy meeting and interacting with Oaxaca's street vendors. We feel that they add greatly to the richness of Oaxaca. Many of their wares, from handwoven table runners and purses to beautifully embroidered blouses, are of the same quality as in the stores. If you buy from a vendor, in many cases you'll be dealing with the same person who made the item, and you can negotiate a good (but respectful) price.

Tipping: The standard rate is 10%. Most restaurants do not include a tip in the bill, but check if you're with a large group. If you spend time at the *zócalo*, you'll be asked for tips by the many strolling musicians. Unless we've been really bothered (for example by an overly loud trombone player) we tip gladly, seeing it as doing our part to support Oaxaca's special *ambiente*. A tip of 5 pesos is adequate; 10 pesos is generous.

Good manners: Most *Oaxaqueños* really do take the time to start an exchange with *"buenos días,"* (good morning), *"buenas tardes,"* (good afternoon), or *"buenas noches,"* (good evening). They'll appreciate it when you do the same. Finish requests or orders with *"por favor"* (please), and respond to help or service with *"gracias"* (thanks) or *"muchas gracias"* (many thanks).

As you leave, you may hear *"que le vaya bien,"* (may it go well for you), to which the proper response is "igualmente," (the same to you).

Movies in Oaxaca: Oaxaca has modern, multi-screen movie theaters located in the large shopping centers southeast of town, Cinepolis and Multimax. These theaters screen first-run movies, although usually a few weeks later than they appear in the U.S. It's a somewhat guilty pleasure for those of us who live or spend a lot of time in Oaxaca to sneak out to see a new movie that we've been hearing about.

Of more interest to many visitors, however, are the **free screenings at Cineclub El Pochote**, at Garcia Vigil 817, (http://elpochote.blogspot.com/), screened Tuesday through Sunday and starting at about 7:00 p.m. In addition to films in Spanish, El Pochote often features art films, documentaries and classics.

Laundry: There are quite a few *lavanderias* — places to get your clothes washed — scattered around Oaxaca. If you need to find one nearby, your best bet is to ask for a recommendation from where you're staying. The only self-service laundromat we've found in Oaxaca is **Lava-max**, at the corner of M. Bravo and Tinoco y Palacios, with a branch in Colonia Reforma at H. Colegio Militar 421. As with most *lavanderias* in Oaxaca, you can drop off your laundry to be done at a reasonable price — around 12 pesos per kilogram (a kilogram is 2.2 pounds) -- but Lava-max will also let you do your own wash at a slightly lower price.

Hair and Nails: For men and women, **Dominique Belleza** at Constitución 110 (501 1811) is a friendly and popular place for haircuts, manicures, and pedicures. **Geminiano Studio de Imagen** at Abasolo 300 (514 8618) is large and modern, offering the same services. A friend came back from a pedicure at Geminiano with nothing but praise for the experience. Perhaps better known is **Londres**, at Morelos 1001 (516 0656), a favorite of well-heeled Oaxacans and many ex-pats. For a precision haircut, the best we've found is by Francisco, at Le Van's salon, Amapolas 1001 in Colonia Reforma (503 0235). Two good places for pedicures are Victoria's Salon at Alianza 216-A in the barrio of Jalatlaco, and Rux Salon at 5 de Mayo near the corner of Murguia in the center. Most of these salons are open from 10am to 7pm, without closing for lunch, daily except Sundays.

Men can get very good **haircuts** from Mauro or Rafael at **Robert's alta peluqueria**, Amapolas 522 in Colonia Reforma (513 5446); open daily except Sunday from 8am to 9pm, closed from 3pm to 5pm. While you're in the neighborhood, drop by **Itanoni**, around the corner on Belisario Dominquez, for breakfast or lunch. If all you need is a good old haircut, try **Peluqueria Trebol** at Constitución # 305 (cellphone 044 951 118 6466), open Monday through Friday 9:30am to 8pm, Saturday 9am to 8pm, Sunday 9am to 3pm.

Internet: Oaxaca has an abundance of internet outlets. Most are functional, although in many cases the computers may be older and slower than you might like. You may also run into non-standard keyboards that can be frustrating.

It seems as though the **@ key** is never where you expect it, and, when found, requires some unusual combination of keystrokes. When in doubt, ask *"¿Como se hace la arroba?"* ("arroba" is the Spanish word for the @ sign).

Inter@ctive Internet, just across from Santo Domingo church at Alcalá 503, is open many hours per day, every day of the week, has lots of clean, well-functioning computers, high-speed connectivity — including wireless -- and is run in a friendly way by Roberto Ramírez and family.

Most cafes in Oaxaca now offer free wireless internet access if you order something to eat or drink. These include **Café Los Cuiles**, in **Plaza de las Virgenes** at Labastida 115, **Nuevo Mundo, La**

Brujula, Gozobi, and Arabia, all described in our **"Coffee"** section. You provide your own laptop, of course.

Oaxaca's beautiful **public library**, at Alcalá 200, offers **free internet service** at the back of the interior patio, and provides the computers. You can also go wireless anywhere in **Llano Park.**.

Source for **low-carb foods:** If you're on an Atkins diet, or just trying to cut back on carbs, you can find low and zero-carb foods at **LOWcarb sin azucar/Le monde sans sucre**, at Berriozabal # 208, in the center (open from 9 a.m. to 2 p.m. and 4 p.m. to 9 p.m., 516-2295. This is a small store with a good idea.

Photography: Oaxaca is endlessly photogenic, but it's worth observing a few caveats. Don't use your flash inside churches or when taking pictures of fine art. Ask permission before taking photos of individuals or small groups of people. *"¿Por favor, me permite tomar una foto?"* Many indigenous people do not want their pictures taken; one lovely old woman very politely explained that she didn't want us to take her soul home with us. However, when people do say yes, you'll take away a much better picture, and leave a much better impression.

You can burn a CD at most internet outlets. For digital prints, we like **Fotografia Alfa Digital** at Fiallo 205, Guerrero 213, or Hidalgo 417. For film, try **Multi Fotos** at J.P. García 601. Both are quick, and work with you to make sure you get good results. Friends have also had good results with digital or film at **Oaxakolor** at Garcia Vigil 106-J, in the center. (Tel. 514 0258).

Camera repairs are not easy here. In a pinch, try the ingeniero fotográfico (photographic engineer) on the second floor at the corner of Galiano and Trujano.

Shoe Repair: For a shoe in need, we recommend **Zapateria La Moda,** at Calle Reforma # 506. Open from 9am to 10pm Monday through Saturday. Abel Méndez Alcázar will fix your shoes if they can be fixed, or let you know if they are beyond repair.

Car Repair: If you're here with a car and it needs work, try **911 Taller Mecanico**, at Vasconcellos 503, off the Calzada de Niños

Heroes near the baseball stadium in the central district of Oaxaca. Jorge Davila will give you prompt, honest, and highly competent service. 515 4675, Cellphone 044 951 187 5337.

Bathrooms: Inevitably there will be times when you want to find a bathroom without having to go back to your hotel. Here is a sampling of locations around town whose bathrooms we have occasionally used without being guests or patrons of the establishment (all are mentioned with addresses herein): 100% Natural; Bar Jardin and restaurant Terranova on the zócalo; the various Italian Coffee Company branches; the Oaxaca Lending Library; and the Hotel Camino Real (go through the lobby and turn left. Look purposeful). Don't try to use the bathrooms in the lobby of the Hotel Marques del Valle unless you're a hotel guest or customer in the restaurant. It can get embarrassing.

Market days—*tianguis*—*días de plaza*

Monday: Miahuatlán
Tuesday: Santa María Atzompa
Wednesday: Etla and Zimatlán
Thursday: Zaachila and Ejutla
Friday: Ocotlán de Morelos
Saturday: markets in Oaxaca
Sunday: Tlacolula

Websites for more information

www.oaxaca-travel.com
www.go-oaxaca.com
www.oaxacalive.com
www.oaxacainfo.com
www.mexonline.com
www.allaboutoaxaca.com
www.oaxacaoaxaca.com
http://oaxaca.gob.mx/sedic/english/e_hypertext2.html
www.ticketbus.com.mx
www.suite101.com/search.cfm?q=Oaxaca
www.peoplesguide.com
www.planeta.com/oaxaca.html

Disappointments!

After considerable thought, we decided that visitors' time in Oaxaca is too precious to waste. So we're listing the few places that, for various reasons, we have found disappointing or unpleasant:

AREEM packing and shipping, Garcia Vigil
Café Alex, Díaz Ordaz
El Topil restaurant, south side of Labastida Park
Fonda Santo Domingo restaurant, 5 de Mayo
La Red restaurant in Colonia Reforma (although their branch on
 Bustamante, south of the *zócalo*, is okay)
Los Pacos restaurant, Abasolo 121
Mayordomo restaurant, 300 block of Alcalá
@lcala internet outlet, Alcalá 206 H

Disclaimer: We make every effort to ensure that this book is accurate and up to date. But as every traveler knows, restaurants come and go, chefs have their off days or their days off, businesses move or close. We hope that what we've written will help you to enjoy your time in Oaxaca. If, as sometimes happens, our suggestions lead you to a boarded-up building or a disappointing meal, please accept our apologies. We welcome your **updates** and constructive **suggestions** at sioaxaca@aol.com.

Viva Oaxaca's Website

For updates on Oaxaca and its surroundings, including news, commentary and many helpful links, or to order copies of *Viva Oaxaca* online, please visit our website, www.si-oaxaca.com.

A Note about Giving

Oaxaca is one of Mexico's poorest states. You'll see many people in need--tiny children selling chewing gum, street musicians, and ancient-looking beggars on the street. Visitors, of course, can respond in whatever way feels right to them. A clear and culturally acceptable way to say "no" is simply to wave your index finger from side to side and break off eye contact.

If you would like to **help people in need** here in a systematic way, we strongly endorse the seven local charitable projects listed below. We value what they are doing and we know first hand that contributions go directly to where they are needed:

Libros para Pueblos (Books for Small Towns) creates and maintains free libraries of high quality children's books in Spanish in *pueblos* in and around Oaxaca. They currently bring the gift of reading to 20,000 children in 40 communities. You can learn more at www.librosparapueblos.com, or at the Oaxaca Lending Library at Pino Suarez 519, just south of Llano park.

Niños Adelante! (Let's Go, Kids!) provides free, fun, English classes and Headstart-style activities to more than 100 Oaxacan children at the Lending Library. Like Libros para Pueblos, this program is very sucessful and is growing rapidly. It's a great way to contribute directly to the Oaxacan community. The Library provides a limited amount of financial assistance, but the program needs much more support since it is growing so rapidly.

Because both of the above programs are part of the Oaxaca Lending Library, **donations are tax-exempt for U.S. taxpayers**. Checks can be made out to the Oaxaca Lending Library Foundation, Inc. (with a note indicating where you want your donation to go). The Library's mailing address in Mexico is APDO 1351, Centro, 68000, Oaxaca, Mexico. In the U.S., checks can be sent to 5443 Drover Drive, San Diego, CA 92115. Or, while in Oaxaca you can come by the library and donate in person.

Albergue Infantil Josefino, A.C. is an orphanage that provides a home and education to orphaned children from throughout the state of Oaxaca. Trusted friends of ours serve on the board or have volunteered here, and vouch for the high quality of services the Albergue provides to hundreds of needy children. If you're in Oaxaca and want to donate, go to the orphanage at Cuitláhuoc # 102, Colonia Ixcotel (513 5700). They will be happy to accept a cash or in-kind donation. In the U.S., a check made out to the Albergue Infantil Josefino may be sent to Gretchen Wirtz, 1640 East 50th St. # 21-C, Chicago, IL 60615-3279.

Procasa Hogar del Niño, A.C. provides a home, education, and other services to orphaned or abandoned boys up to age 15. Their house at Arista # 103 usually shelters from 12 to 15 children. ProcasaHogar is always in need of donations. You can contact the president, Rosa Alba Palacios de Vargas, at 514 5923 or on her cellphone, 044 951 127 9045. If you're in Oaxaca and want to donate, call her a day in advance to set up an appointment at the shelter. She'll be there to show you arround, accept your donation, and give you a receipt.

Estancia Fraternidad, A.C. Oaxaca's public hospitals and clinics are underfunded and understaffed. As a result, family members of patients must provide their food and help care for them. The Estancia Fraternidad provides shelter, food and support to poor families who have come to Oaxaca from distant pueblos to care for a hospitalized family member. Since 1991, The Estancia has helped nearly 700,000 family members. In the U.S. and Canada checks can be made out to St. Joseph's Church, and sent to Robert Buckley, 2730 Heather View Circle, Marion, Iowa 52302. In Oaxaca, you can drop by their offices at Las Rosas # 723 in Colonia Reforma (513 1930, open from 8am to 10pm daily; www.geocities.com/estanciaoaxaca). Donations are tax deductible in the U.S.

Casa Hogar Hijos de la Luna provide much needed care and services to the children of sex workers in Oaxaca. This unique organization can always use financial and volunteer help. To contribute in any way, contact Sra. Maria del Socorro Ramírez de Larracilla, known as Doña Coco, the program's director, at (951) 132 1687, or email her at *contacto@hijosdelaluna.org*.

Fundación En Via is bringing the proven benefits of microcredit or microfinance to the women of Oaxaca. Applying the Nobel-Prize-winning ideas of Muhammed Yunus, En Via provides small loans—on the order of a few hundred dollars–to local women to help them start or build their businesses. They've helped 130 women so far. Contributors who have gone on En Via tours to meet the women they are helping have been deeply moved. You can learn more about En Via's work at *www.envia.org*, or email them at *info@envia.org*.

A Final Word

If you're like us, your first visit to Oaxaca will not be your last. In the end, we came to see that it's not the stately colonial buildings, the ancient, echoing ruins, the savory food, or the colorful crafts that keep calling us back, but the vitality and warmth of the *Oaxaqueños* themselves. "*Hasta la proxima,*" we promise ourselves; "Until the next time."

¡Que disfrute! — Enjoy!

Robert Adler and Jo Ann Wexler

As a service to our readers, we provide frequent and continuing updates to *Viva Oaxaca* at:
http://www.si-oaxaca.com/viva_oaxaca_updates.htm

We welcome your questions or comments at: sioaxaca@aol.com.

Front cover photo by Mario Garza Elizondo
Email: margarel@gmail.com

Cover design by Kim Elinski
Email: mexikim@hotmail.com

INDEX

Abastos (wholesale market) 62,63,68,84
Academia de Baile (dance school) 73
Aeromexico 64
Aerotoucan 65,69
Aerovega 69
Agencia de Viajes Marques del Valle 66
Aguilar, family of ceramicists 22
Airlines 64
Airport shuttle 65
Aitana hotel 29
Alamo Rental Cars 69
Albergue Infantil Josefino 93
Alcalá, the 4
Alebrijes 22,23,26,58,59,60
Almuerzo 32
Alvarez Bravo Photographic Center 14
Amara 59
Amate Books 68,85
Ambar (amber) 59,63
Ambulance 80
Andador turistico, 4
Ángeles, Claudia. (Spanish teacher) 71
Angeles, Jacobo and Maria 23,60
Another Oaxaca (tours) 67
Apartments for rent 85
Arabia Café 52,90
Arrazola 24,26,58
Art 63
Arte Biulu 63
Arte de Oaxaca 63
Arte de Oaxaca gallery 22
Artesanías Cosijo 59
Artesans Market 62
Atlantida vans 69
Atzompa 8,57
Aurobics Fitness Gym 73
Autobuses Turisticos (to Monte Alban) 67
Aviacsa 64
Avolar Airlines 64
Ayuuk (Sierra Mixe handicrafts) 61
Azteca Airlines 65
Azucena Zapoteca restaurant 23
Azul, hotel and restaurant 37

Bar del Jardin 41
Barber 89

Bargaining 58,63
Barro negro (black pottery) 57
Barro rojo (red pottery) 57
Barro verde (green pottery) 57
Bathrooms 91
Bautista, Flor (Spanish teacher) 70
Beauty 88
Becari Language School 70
Belber Jimenez Museum 14
Bengali (woven goods) 62
Benito Juarez (town) 74
Benito Juarez covered market 61,63,84
Benito Juárez home 15,54
Bicycles 74
Bii Daüü, Zapotec Weaving Cooperative 20
Bilingual library 85
Bird experts 67,75
Black Coffee & Gallery 52
Black pottery 57
Books/bookstores 85
Bor Bon cafe 52
Breakfast 34,37,38,42,43,45,51,52,53
Bug in the Rug 19
Building J 17,18
Bus route maps 66

Cabrera, Pilar (cooking classes) 72
Café Café 55
Café Central 55
cafe de la olla 52
Café del Teatro 52
Café Gecko 51
Café La Antigua 51
Café Los Cuiles 89
Cafe Oaxaqueño (Oaxacan coffee) 52
Cafetería Bander Burger 43
Cafetería La Principal 45
Caldo de Piedra restaurant 49
Calendar of events 12
Calipso Fitness Center 74
Camino Real hotel 4,56,84
Candela 55,73
Car repair 90
Carmen Alto 6
Carmen Alto church 54
Carrizal, Fredy (biologist, bird expert) 75
Casa Adobe B&B 27
CASA art center 26,50

Casa Catrina hotel 29
Casa Colonial B&B 27
Casa Conzatti hotel 29
Casa Crespo (B&B, cooking classes) 72
Casa Crespo restaurant 37
Casa de Cantera 56
Casa de la Ciudad 13
Casa de las Bugambilias B&B 30
Casa de los Frailes hotel 30
Casa de Maria Lombardo restaurant 44
Casa de Sierra Azul hotel 28
Casa del Angel 57
Casa del Sotano hotel 29
Casa Elpidia restaurant 43
Casa Hogar Hijos de la Luna 94
Casa Linda B&B 31
Casa Machaya B&B 27
Casa Oaxaca 4,34
Casa Oaxaca Café 37
Casa Oaxaca hotel 27
Casa Oaxaca restaurant 33
Casa Vertiz hotel 30
Cathedral 4,
Cemetery 8
Cena (evening meal) 32
Centro de las Artes de San Agustín 26
Centro Fotografico Alvarez Bravo 14
Chapulines (grasshoppers) 25
Chavez, Federico 20
Ché Gaucho restaurant 35
Chefi restaurant 50
Chepil 32
Chimalli 59
China Beijing restaurant 44
Chocolate (Oaxacan) 16,63
Christmas Eve 10
Christmas season 9
Church, Ocotlan's painted 22
Cielito Lindo 55
Cinnabon 52
Classes 69,72
Climate 4,
Clinics 80,81
Colectivos (shared taxis) 68
Colonia Reforma 66
Comalá restaurnat 45
Comedor El Tule 49,61
Comida 32

Comida corrida 41 ff
Comida Economica Isabel 42
Continental Airlines 64
Continental—Istmo tours 66,74
Conzatti park 54
Cooking classes 69,72,73
Cooking, prehispanic 73
Corazon Zapoteco 60
Coyotepec 57
Crafts and folkart 31,
Cuilápan, ex-convent 24,26

Dainzu 21
Dance classes 69,73
Danza de la Pluma 6
Day of the Dead 7
De la Parra hotel 28
Dentists 82,83
Dia de los Muertos 7
Disappointments 92
Doctors 81
Dominican Route 26
Don Juanito restaurant chain 10
Don Pizzotte pizzeria 44
Doña Inez 53
Donations/recommended charities 92 ff
Donde está mi Crepa? Restaurant 43
Downs, Lila 56
Drivers 67
Duran, Gisela Camarillo 57

Ejutla 84
Ejutla de Crespo 23
El Andariego restaurant 42
El Buen Gourmet cafeteria 42
El Camino Real hotel 27
El Camino Real hotel 27
El Ché restaurant 35
El Encanto 20
El Encuentro 6,
El Importador restaurant 42
El Jolgorio (guide to art and events) 63
El Morocco restaurant 45
El Nagual 59
El Pochote (free movies) 88
El Sazon de la Abuela restaurant 50
El Tipico restaurant 39
El Tule 19,46,49,61

Embroidery 58,61
Emergencies 80,86
Epazote 32
Epicuro Cafe Bistrot Italian restaurant 44
Español Interactivo 71
Estancia Fraternidad 94
Ethnic groups 84
Ethnobotanic Gardens 12,83
Etla 8,50,84
Etnico Textiles 60
Europecar 69
Exercise 73

Farmacias de Ahorro (pharmacy) 78
Federico 61
Festival de Otoño 7
Filigrana (filigree) 59
Film Festival 9
Fire 86
First-class bus station (ADO) 69
Folkart and crafts 31,
Fortín hill 6,
Free Bar 55
Fuego y Sazón restaurant 38
Fundación En Via (microcredit) 94

Galeria 910 63
Galeria Indigo 63
Galeria Quetzalli 63
García López sisters (embroidery) 61
Gardens, Ethnobotanic 12
Giving/recommended charities 92 ff
Gonzalez, Pablo (guide) 67
Good Friday 6
Gozobi cafe 51,90
Gratemalan crafts 60
Green pottery 57
Guapinol 59
Guelagüetza 6,56
Guelagüetza auditorium 6
Guelagüetza dance shows 56
Guiarte (guide to Oaxacan art) 63
Guides 67

Hacienda/Restaurante Santa Marta 48
Hair and nails 88
Haircuts 89
Harp, Susana 56

Hecmafer Bazar Artesanal 59
Hertz 69
Hierba santa 32
Hierve el Agua 18
Hiitlacoche 32
Hipotesis 55
Holy Week 5,
Horseback riding 75
Horsebackmexico 75
Hospitals 80,81
Hostal Casa del Sótano 29
Hosteria de Alcalá restaurant 38
Hotel Aitana 29
Hotel Aurora 32
Hotel Azucenas 31
Hotel Casa Vertiz 30,51
Hotel de la Parra 28
Hotel Las Golondrinas 31
Hotel Las Mariposas 30
Hotel Marqués del Valle 29
Hotel Parador San Miguel 29
Hotel Rivera del Angel 67
Hotel Victoria 28,84
Huatulco 68

Ice Cream 13
ICI-Instituto de Communicación Intl. 70
ICO-Instituto Cultural Oaxaca 69
Institute of Graphic Arts (IAGO) 14
Instituto Oaxaqueño de las Artesanías 58
Intercambio (English-Spanish) 70,71,85
Internet 89,90
Italian Coffee Company 52,
Itanoni restaurant 39,89

Jacobo Angeles, master carver 23,60
Jardín Conzatti 54

La Biznaga restaurant 35
La Brujula cafe 51,90
La Caballeriza restaurant 48
La Cafeteria restaurant 41
La Calenda 61
La Cantinita 55
La Capilla restaurant 25,50
La Casa de las Artesanías 58
La Casa de los Abuelos B&B 31
La Casa de Maria 56

La Cucaracha 55
La Encantada Orquideario 19
La Escondida buffet 46
La Hormiga sandwiches 54
La Jicara restaurant and bookstore 39
La Mano Mágica 59
La Marquesita 59
La Nueva Babel 55
La Palapa de Raúl restaurant 49
La Parroquia 55
La Pasión 53
La Plaza (artesanías) 58
La Salamandra 55
La Tentacion 55
La Union (carvers) 58
Labastida park 63
Lambityeco 21
Las Golondrinas 31
Las Mariposas hotel 30
Las Quince Letras restaurant 39
Laundry 88
Learning Center, the 31
Library of Oaxaca 14,90
Library, bilingual 85
Libros Amate 68,85
Libros para Pueblos 93
Linen clothing 60
Linguistic groups 84
Llano Park 16,90
Location (of Oaxaca) 84
Lopez, Josefina 20
Los Almendros restaurant 39
Los Anzulejos restaurant 37
Los Combinados taqueria 40
Los Danzantes (figures) 17
Los Danzantes restaurant 34
Los Naranjos restaurant 42
Los Nubes cafe/restaurant 51
Low-carbohydrate foods 90

Mail 87
Manners 88
Manolo Nieves ice cream 13
Manos Indígenas de Oaxaca 57
Maps 47,48,68
Marco Polo restaurant 37
Market, artisans' 16
Market, organic 17

Market, outdoor 16,84
Markets, covered 16
Markets, outdoor weekly 19,23,24
MARO (women artisans coop) 58
Marqués del Valle hotel 29
Massage 57
Meat, how well done 33
Medical doctors 81,82
Megapilates Estudio (Pilates) 73
Mendoza, Arnulfo 19
Mendoza, Loty (San Miguel Shoes) 61
Mercado de las Artesanías 62
Meson del Olivo restaurant 36
Mexicana Airlines 64
Mezcal 4,
Mezcal 4,6,35,75 ff
Mezzaluna Ristorante 44
Mia Arroz Chinese restaurant 50
Microcredit 94
Microdyn (disinfectant) 80
Mitla 18,84
Mitla, guide to 18
Mixteca market 62
Mole 32,63,64
Money 85
Monte Albán 17,67,84
Monte Albán, guide to 17
Morales, Rudolfo 22
Mountain bikes 75
Mountain biking 75
Movies 88
Museo de Pintores Oaxaqueños 15
Museo del Palacio 15
Museo Estatal de Arte Popular 24
Museo Rufino Tamayo 13
Museo Textil de Oaxaca 13
Museum at Soledad Basilica 13
Museum Belber Jimenez 14
Museum of Contemporary Art (MACO) 14
Museum of Oaxacan Cultures 12
Museum of Oaxacan Painters 15,22
Museum, Ocotlan 22,23
Music, CDs 87
Music, classical 6
Music, early 8

Namaste massage 57
Nieves, SeZora (temazcal) 57

Night of the Radishes 10
Nightspots 55
Niños Adelante! 93
Noche de Luces 11
Noche de Rabanos 10
Nuevo Mundo (coffee) 50,89

Oaxaca Lending Library 71,85
Oaxaca Ollin B&B 27
Oaxaca Raizes 60
Oaxaca Spanish Magic 70
Ocotlan 21,58,68,84
Oja santa 32
Olachea, Laura (Spanish teacher) 71
Ollin Tlahtoalli language school 71
Organ festival 8
Organic market 17
Organs, antique 9
Orquideario La Encantada 19

Packing & Shipping 87
Palace of Government Museum 15
Pan & Co. 52
Pan dulce 52
Panteón General 8
Parque Juárez 16
Pharmacies 81
Photography 90
Plaza de las Virgines 89
Plaza del Valle 66
Plaza los Geranios 60
Plaza Oaxaca 66
Plaza San Jeronimo 52
Plazuela de Carmen Alto 59
Police 86
Political activity 86
Population 84
Posada Casa Oaxaca 27
Post Office 87
Pottery, black 24,57
Pottery, etched 58
Procasa Hogar del Niño 94
Procession of Silence 5,
Puebla 68
Pueblos Mancomunados 74
Puerto Angel 68
Puerto Escondido 68,69

Rabanos 10
Ramirez, Luis (driver) 67
Red pottery 57
Rental cars 69
Reviews, restaurant 33
Ropa tipica (traditional clothing) 60,61
Rufino Tamayo Museum 13
Rugs, woven 19,
Ruta Dominicana 26

Safety, security 85 ff
Samaritana 6
San Bartolo Coyotepec 24
San Felipe del Agua 8
San Martin Tilcajete 23,58
San Miguel shoes 60
Santa Ana del Valle 21
Santa Marta buffet 48
Santiago, Roque Antonio (bird expert) 75
Santo Domingo church 4,12,83
Santo Domingo Plaza 60
Santo Tomás Jalieza 23,58
Seasons of My Heart (cooking school) 72
Second-class bus transport 68,74
Semana Santa 5,
Servicio Express vans 69
Shoe repair 90
Sierra Mixe 61
Sierra Morena 60
SierraNorte (eco-tourism) 74
Sitio ADO (taxi stand) 66,68
Sitio Alameda (taxi stand) 66,68
Soledad basilica 7,9,13
Sonrya Galeria
Spanish classes 69 ff
SpanishClassesOaxaca 71
State Band of Oaxaca 4,55,84
State Marimba Band 55
State Museum of Popular Art 24
Stone Soup restaurant 49
Street vendors 87
Suarez, Silvia 60

Tacos Alvaro 40
Tamales 11,32,54
Tapetes, woven 19
Taxi Express 66
Taxis 26,38,46,49,65,66,67,68

TAYU restaurant 42
Teatro Macedonio Alcalá 6, 14,52,56,84
Telephone calling information 27
Temazcal 56,57
Tempero 60
Templo San Agustin 54
Teotitlán del Valle 19,45,58,84
Terra Quemada 60
Terranova restaurant 41
Textile Museum of Oaxaca 13
Thai food 43
Tianguis 19,21,84
Ticketbus 69
Tierraventura (eco-tourism) 74
Tipping 87
Tlacolula 19,50,84
Tlamanalli Restaurant 21,45,84
Tlapazola 58
Tlayudas 32,33,49,53,54
Tourist Office 66
Tours, culinary 72
Tours, Walking 13
Transportes de Ocotlán 68
Transportes Terrestre (airport shuttle) 65
Travel Agencies (for tours) 66
Travel alert (U.S. Dept. of State) 86
Trilling, susana (cooking school) 72
Tule 19
Turismo Aventura (eco-tourism) 75
Tuxtepec 8

UNESCO World Heritage 4,
Updates to Viva Oaxaca 95

Vans (to the Pacific Coast) 69
Vasquez, Isaac 19
Veracruz 68
Veterinarians 83
Viajes Paradiso 67
Vida Nueva, Zapotec women's cooperative 20
Vinigulaza language academy 70
Virgin de la Soledad 9
Vista Hermosa 26
Vivaaerobus 65
Volaris Airlines 65

Walking tours 13
Water 79
Website 92

Xoxocotlán 8

Yagul 21
Yu Ne Nisa restaurant 40

Zaachila 8,24,50,84
Zaachila, archaeological site 25
Zócalo 4,10,11,15,16,28,29.31,54,55.57,58,63,83

100 Percent Natural restaurant 45
1254 Marco Polo restaurant 37
20th of November covered market 61,84

NOTES

Made in the USA
Lexington, KY
01 September 2011